CHANNEL THE CHARGE: PARENTING CHILDREN WITH ADHD

PRACTICAL WAYS TO: HARNESS ENERGY, BOOST SELF-ESTEEM, NURTURE EMOTIONAL GROWTH, AND STRENGTHEN FAMILY BONDS

ABIGAIL SHEPARD

© **Copyright 2024 – All rights reserved.**

The content contained within this book may not be reproduced, duplicated, or transmitted without direct written permission from the author or the publisher.

Under no circumstances will any blame or legal responsibility be held against the publisher, or author, for any damages, reparations, or monetary loss due to the information contained within this book, either directly or indirectly.

Legal Notice:

This book is copyright protected. It is only for personal use. You cannot amend, distribute, sell, use, quote, or paraphrase any part, or the content within this book, without the consent of the author or publisher.

Disclaimer Notice:

Please note that the information contained within this document is for educational and entertainment purposes only. All effort has been executed to present accurate, up-to-date, reliable, and complete information. No warranties of any kind are declared or implied. Readers acknowledge that the author is not engaged in the rendering of legal, financial, medical, or professional advice. The content within this book has been derived from various sources. Please consult a licensed professional before attempting any techniques outlined in this book.

By reading this document, the reader agrees that under no circumstances is the author responsible for any losses, direct or indirect, that are incurred as a result of the use of the information contained within this document, including, but not limited to, errors, omissions, or inaccuracies.

CONTENTS

Introduction	5
1. GAINING A NEW PERSPECTIVE	9
What Is ADHD?	10
ADHD Misconceptions	12
ADHD in Boys and Girls	14
Diagnosing ADHD	16
ADHD Therapy and Medications	18
The Advantages	22
Summary	24
Journaling for Self-Reflection	25
2. MUST-HAVE PARENTING SKILLS	27
Challenges of Parenting a Child with ADHD	28
Adjusting Parenting Style	32
Must-Have Parenting Skills	36
Journaling for Self-Reflection	42
3. OVERCOME BEHAVIORAL CHALLENGES	43
What Triggers Challenging Behaviors?	44
Hyperactivity and Impulsivity	48
Inattentiveness	51
Tantrums	55
Discipline Strategies	56
Create Your Rewards Chart	58
Journaling for Self-Reflection	59
4. BUILDING BLOCKS OF SUCCESS	61
Routine and Structure	62
Establishing an Effective Routine at Home	63
ADHD-Friendly Environment	72
Time Blindness and Time Management	74
Create a Visual Schedule	76
Journaling for Self-Reflection	77

5. CULTIVATE PHYSICAL WELL-BEING — 79
   Nutrition — 79
   Sleep — 83
   Physical Activity — 85
   Five-Day Meal Plan — 87
   Journaling for Self-Reflection — 88

6. EMOTIONAL RESILIENCE BEYOND MEASURE — 91
   Emotional Dysregulation and ADHD — 92
   Emotional Regulation Strategies — 94
   Mindfulness — 96
   Fostering Emotional Resilience — 98
   Journaling for Self-Reflection — 100

7. WORDS THAT CONNECT — 101
   Communication Challenges — 102
   Active Listening — 103
   Parent-Child Harmony — 106
   Journaling for Self-Reflection — 108

8. ADVOCATE FOR YOUR CHILD'S EDUCATION — 109
   Individualized Education Programs (IEPs) — 110
   504 Plan — 113
   Establishing Parent-School Partnerships — 115
   Education Starts at Home — 116
   Journaling for Self-Reflection — 118

9. HARNESS THE ADHD SUPERPOWERS — 121
   Hyperfocus — 121
   Creativity — 123
   High Energy — 124
   Building Their Self-Esteem — 125
   Journaling for Self-Reflection — 126

10. FAMILY FORTITUDE — 129
    How ADHD Plays into Parent/Child Relationships — 130
    Balancing Sibling Relationships — 131
    Strengthening Partnerships as Parents — 133
    Journaling for Self-Reflection — 134

    Conclusion — 137
    References — 141

INTRODUCTION

 The moment you begin to actively discover the amazing personhood of your child, parenting starts to feel like less of a burden and more of an adventure.

— ANGELA PRUESS

No one said parenting was easy, but they also didn't tell you how difficult it would be to parent a child with ADHD. Parenting is undoubtedly the toughest job in the world; you want the best for your child, to see them happy and thriving, yet every action you take almost feels like it's to their detriment. You're stuck in this cycle of guilt and self-doubt, where everything you do feels wrong. Scolding your child for continuously losing their pens, pencils, and sweaters feels criminal. Attempting to sneak nutritious food into their diets as they freak out in panic and disgust is exhausting. Teaching them how to not interrupt and just focus on one activity feels impossible. But then, there's that glimpse of hope, where they're happy, confident, and excited to tackle anything that enters their path.

Parenting truly is a journey, one where you and your child learn to grow together. It's a tough job, but, oh boy, it's the best one out there. Rewarding, fulfilling, and heartening couldn't even define how spectacular it is to parent a child with ADHD. I know you're probably reading this in confusion and pulling your hair out from the chaos surrounding you, but trust me, with the right tools and strategies in place, parenthood gets a million times better. In fact, there's a whole new side to parenting that you have yet to discover. On this journey, you will reach new levels that require a lot of love, patience, and understanding. We're going to be ditching those traditional standards for parenting and starting a new chapter.

If you're reading this book, chances are you've blamed yourself for your child's behavior more times than you could possibly remember—that emotional rollercoaster of guilt, shame, and blame really is a nightmare! As you know, ADHD comes with a lot of struggles; it's almost like you're stuck in a perpetual battle attempting to manage your child's symptoms of ADHD as if they were within your control, to begin with. Despite all the energy, love, and encouragement you pour into your child's life, you're left feeling overwhelmed, stressed, and probably even hopeless. I'm here to tell you that it's okay; what you are feeling is a natural response to the pressure placed on your shoulders. It is not your fault that you haven't been given the right tools and strategies to help both you and your child live a life full of joy and simplicity. Today, that's all going to change.

You and your child deserve to live a life where your relationships, friendships, and family don't bear the consequences of ADHD—a life where your child grows and learns with their peers, and you can sit back in confidence, knowing that they'll be okay. I know firsthand how heartbreaking it can be to see your little one isolated from the world, witnessing children their age find your child unrelatable. Making friends, maintaining relationships, and even participating in social activities can feel like a nightmare for your child, even if they're not so little anymore. No matter how much you push, encourage, or hold their hand, friendships are a source of stress, tension, and struggle for the entire family.

We could unpack every downfall of ADHD—struggles with academics, troubling symptoms, fear and anxiety, and even the financial burden of getting support—but that's not what I'm here for. Together, we are going to change the narrative. In this new chapter of your life, we're going to be waving goodbye to negativity and welcoming positivity; after all, this will help us massively on our parenting journey. Now, I'm not saying that from this moment on, everything will be sunshine and rainbows; we will have a lot of bumps and hurdles to face. With the help of holistic approaches, a comprehensive range of strategies and solutions, and personalized interventions tailored to your child's unique needs, facing daily challenges will be a breeze.

Get ready to ditch those feelings of shame, guilt, and self-doubt. This new step in parenthood is all about empowerment and confidence. With each decision you make and every action you take, you'll know that it is for the betterment of your child, to help them grow and develop into an incredible individual. You'll get to witness a transformation in your child that is so big and impactful that the entire family dynamic will be enhanced with a renewed sense of hope and optimism for the future.

I know it almost sounds too good to be true, but I promise you this is achievable. With real-life case studies, authentic advice, and practical solutions, you will gain access to a wide range of strategies beyond medication and behavior modification. Picture it as creating your own personalized ADHD toolkit to support your family.

You've already taken the first step; opening the first page and reading this far means you are ready to improve your family's life. Going through the ups and downs of ADHD alone is far too much for a parent to handle; it's okay to want help and to need it, ask for it, and take it. Raising a child takes a village, so it's okay if you need a little helping hand—even if it comes from a book!

Let's start this journey together and unlock the secrets to making your child's ADHD their superpower!

GAINING A NEW PERSPECTIVE

> " I wish people simply knew that ADHD is so much more than just "being hyper."
>
> — S.S.

As children grow, they go through heaps of changes and experience a mountain of pressure and expectation, all while battling a variety of hormones and feelings they've never felt before. As a parent who understands ADHD, I've come to realize that hyperactivity may be one of the most frustrating symptoms. And no, this isn't because the child is bouncing off the walls with excitement and creativity but rather due to the misconceptions surrounding it, especially when other parents chime in. If you've ever heard: "Oh, they're all over the place. It's like they can't sit still for a second! Must be a real handful to deal with," you'll know exactly what I'm talking about.

While we can't change the perspectives of others, we can change our own. There is so much more to ADHD than meets the eye. Let's begin this chapter by shining some light and love on the beauty hidden within ADHD!

WHAT IS ADHD?

While ADHD in children has been commonly confused with "naughtiness" or "bad parenting," this viewpoint isn't accurate. ADHD is a neurodevelopmental condition; in fact, it's one of the most common disorders today. It is a chronic condition, meaning it can't be fixed and will impact the individual from childhood all the way to adulthood and old age. However, the degree of intensity can vary from person to person, with typical symptoms affecting emotions, behavior, and learning ability.

All children experience difficulty with paying attention, listening to instructions, and completing tasks. But, for a child with ADHD, it's a bit more complex and severe than this; their struggle is more persistent and continuous, leading to a range of issues with academics, social situations, and behavior. Typically, your child should fall into one of three categories of ADHD:

- **Inattentive:** If you've ever spoken to your child and questioned whether they're even listening, then they may have inattentive ADHD. Inattentive children are easily distracted; they can be watching TV for one minute when a fly passes by, and just like that, they are in the kitchen zooming around, looking for their next activity. Starting one activity and ditching it for something new and exciting is a recurring theme. They may also commonly miss details, daydream, or dawdle around. Listening to

directions and following through with tasks is practically impossible for them.
- **Hyperactive-impulsive:** Every child has energy, but when this energy doesn't seem to tire out, they may have hyperactive-impulsive ADHD. Children with hyperactivity tend to be very fidgety, touching anything they can get their hands on. They may also appear restless and struggle to sit still or stay quiet, even when an adult is talking. Usually, they make careless mistakes without realizing it, fail to think before acting, and rush through activities, tasks, and conversations. On the flip side, their impulsivity can make urges such as pushing and grabbing seem irresistible. The famous idiom "a bull in a china shop" defines them pretty well!
- **Combined:** Just as the name suggests, combined ADHD is when a child has a mix of both hyperactive-impulsive and inattentive symptoms. It is where both types of ADHD are present at the same time.

Keep in mind that the intensity and appearance of symptoms can change over time, especially when little ones are growing or when tweens and teens are going through those fundamental years of adolescence.

In children with ADHD, a part of the brain known as the prefrontal cortex is significantly smaller. This is one of the reasons why managing emotions, resisting urges, and controlling outbursts is so difficult for them. According to research conducted by Wilkins (2024), a variety of studies have also demonstrated that there may be differences in brain functioning in children with ADHD. An important network in the brain that's typically not active during tasks and activities is highly active in children with ADHD. This could be the answer as to why paying and maintaining attention feels virtually impossible during homework time or at school.

It's also important to note that there is a huge imbalance in chemicals like dopamine and norepinephrine in an ADHD brain. With such low levels of these essential chemicals, feelings such as satisfaction and motivation, as well as actions such as making a decision, can become ten times harder. This is why it is fundamental that we give our children the correct tools and strategies for ADHD, so they can create a successful future where they achieve their goals and ambitions.

ADHD MISCONCEPTIONS

An essential part of this journey will include separating facts from fiction. This is especially important for individuals with ADHD, as there is an overload of false information, shame, and misconceptions surrounding the condition. I'm not sure about you, but I definitely don't want my child to grow up in an environment where they believe that their ADHD isn't worthy of treatment, acknowledgment, or respect. Enough of the chit-chat; let's get to blasting this hurtful misconception into space!

ADHD Is the Result of Poor Parenting

As a parent who wants the absolute best for their child, this one hits deep. When a child bounces off the walls, interrupts others, and doesn't listen to instructions, others might jump to the conclusion that ADHD is the result of bad parenting. However, this is very far from the truth, as ADHD is a neurodevelopmental disorder. The condition starts in the brain and is influenced by an imbalance of chemicals and brain functioning.

Keep in mind that traditional parenting methods typically don't work for children with ADHD either. As parents, we have to adapt and find unique strategies that fit the needs of our children. For some of us, this may even involve biting our tongues and excusing others for being misinformed about ADHD!

ADHD Is a Childhood Issue and Will Go Away

ADHD can change over time; its intensity and appearance can alter at any given moment. However, it does not simply disappear. For instance, a child with ADHD may experience hyperactive-impulsive symptoms where they feel urges to interrupt others; as a teen, this may manifest into feeling internally jittery and uncomfortable.

As children grow, they go through heaps of changes and experience a mountain of pressure and expectation, all while battling a variety of hormones and feelings they've never felt before. We must allow them space and time to discover who they are and how their ADHD plays a part in this.

ADHD Only Occurs in Boys

According to the Centers for Disease Control and Prevention (2022), twice as many boys are diagnosed with ADHD. While it's easy to assume that women simply don't have ADHD, bear in mind that medical research and clinical trials have evolved and progressed only in the past fifty to sixty years. Before then, most trials were conducted on men. This means that many women have lived life thinking that ADHD can't happen to them or that medical professionals haven't had the right equipment to diagnose women, as criteria are based on the opposite gender. Additionally, women internalize their symptoms of ADHD, making it harder for others to spot the signs. Don't worry; we'll take a closer look at this soon!

While many more myths surrounding ADHD exist, always give others the benefit of the doubt. As a parent to a child with ADHD, it's your job to represent the beauty behind the condition. Teach others and guide them toward a more positive outlook. Step by step, we'll be able to change the narrative and build a welcoming space for our little ones (even if they're not so little!).

ADHD IN BOYS AND GIRLS

Approximately 13 percent of boys are diagnosed with ADHD compared to about 6 percent of girls, according to the Centers for Disease Control and Prevention (2022). I know: It's shocking. The important thing to remember is that this doesn't imply that women are less likely to have ADHD. The reality behind this statistic is that ADHD criteria are outdated and tailored toward boys.

Typically, females demonstrate inattentive symptoms, which are hard to notice and not so obvious to the eye. Girls are also really good at developing compensatory adaptive behaviors and coping strategies that easily mask their symptoms. Picture this as making a huge mess on the floor but placing a rug over it to mask everything underneath. Generally, women have huge expectations placed on their shoulders to act polite, do well in life, and be independent while being the perfect picture of femininity. Whether they're conscious of it or not, they may be feeling a need to suppress their symptoms of ADHD, making the diagnostic journey a challenging task. Plus, when women do seek out a diagnosis, they're commonly misdiagnosed for depression and anxiety as a result of their less disruptive and obvious symptoms.

To put it simply, boys display the "typical" idea of ADHD: hyperactivity, disruption, and impulsiveness. All of those symptoms are loud and right in front of your face. On the other hand, girls experience an internal battle of daydreaming, feeling intense emotions, and struggling to stay seated. These symptoms are easy to dismiss and don't raise concern from others. Below, you'll find a table that breaks down the different signs and symptoms of ADHD in boys and girls:

	Boys	**Girls**
Signs and Symptoms of ADHD	• Impulsivity • Emotions that don't fit the situation and potentially lead to aggression • Difficulty staying still • Frequent interruption of others during any activity • Excessive talking	• Struggles with listening • Low self-esteem • High anxiety • Poor academics • Inattentive symptoms • Frequent need for extra help with activities like homework • Problems with executive functioning, including short-term memory, self-control, organization, and time management

While we may not want to admit it, after decades of misconstrued information, we have all subconsciously created an idea of ADHD, one that involves boys being the picture-perfect image. As we continue to learn and inform ourselves, it's important that we spread awareness and raise children who understand the importance of equality within ADHD diagnosis. After all, cultivating awareness will build a future where your child's condition is accepted for what it truly is: a superpower!

DIAGNOSING ADHD

Receiving an ADHD diagnosis for your child can feel extremely overwhelming; believe me, I've been there and experienced the stress of it. Well, that was until I reached out to the right healthcare professionals and realized how simple it really was.

A diagnosis is incredibly valuable for so many reasons; not only does it offer your child an opportunity to understand themselves further, but it also provides an answer as to why they're feeling certain emotions. Think about it: Your child is surrounded by peers and children their age, five days a week for nearly all year, and they're bound to feel out of place now and then. Hence, catching those negative thoughts and feelings, such as "I'm lazy, stupid, or horrible," is important before they become obsessive. Plus, understanding what sets them apart from the crowd at an early age allows you more time to build a positive outlook on how beautiful their condition is. Your entire family will be able to build them up, empower them, and set your child up for the future they deserve.

Receiving a diagnosis also opens the door for treatment; whether it's therapy or medication, you and your child will be able to make a well-informed decision on what is best for their emotional and physical well-being. Depending on where you live, you may also receive special support from your child's school, such as regular visits with the school counselor, extra time on projects and work, or other special considerations.

Typically, you'll be able to receive an ADHD diagnosis from the following types of medical professionals:

- **Psychiatrist:** A psychiatrist is highly trained in nearly every condition concerning the brain, especially ADHD. They're also able to diagnose medication and treatment. However, this usually comes at a large cost, with a single hourly appointment costing around $200. Keep in mind that they're not trained in counseling, so if you're looking for day-to-day advice and effective strategies, they may not be the right doctor for you.
- **Psychologist:** A psychologist has a great understanding of how the mind functions and can diagnose ADHD. Plus, they're trained in counseling and more affordable, making them the perfect option for a long-term holistic approach to treatment. Since psychologists only have a baseline amount of knowledge, they do have to refer to other sources, such as an MRI or screenings for diagnosis. Additionally, they cannot prescribe medication and will most likely refer you to a doctor or psychiatrist.
- **Family Doctor:** Your family doctor should know about ADHD, but they will likely lack extensive knowledge. The upside is that they're familiar with your child and their medical history, they can prescribe affordable medication, and you might find it easier to make an appointment with them. However, be prepared for a rushed and not-so-accurate diagnosis, as family doctors are usually jam-packed.
- **Neurologist:** A neurologist is a highly trained professional specializing in the brain and central nervous system. One advantage is that they'll examine the entirety of your child's mind and diagnose any type of condition or disorder, such as seizures. The disadvantage is that they are expensive, use equipment that isn't really necessary for a diagnosis, and will inevitably refer you to a psychologist.

Once you've found the right doctor for your child, you will begin the diagnosis process, where your doctor will check if your child meets the following criteria for ADHD:

- Symptoms manifest in two or more settings, like home, school, and social environments, resulting in some level of impairment.
- For children aged four to seventeen, a minimum of six symptoms should be discernible.
- For individuals aged seventeen and above, a minimum of five symptoms should be discernible.
- Symptoms significantly hinder your child's functioning in various daily activities, including academics, family and peer relationships, and group engagements like sports.
- The onset of symptoms predates the age of twelve, though they may not be recognized as ADHD symptoms until later.
- Symptoms persist for over six months.

Bear in mind that your doctor may also want to reach out to teachers or additional family members. They may check school reports and academic history and conduct a variety of questionnaires and conversations with your child.

ADHD THERAPY AND MEDICATIONS

So, you've received an ADHD diagnosis and want the best for your child but don't really know what steps to take moving forward. Don't worry, I've got your back. Let's break down two simple and effective types of treatment for ADHD:

Therapy

If you're looking for a holistic approach to treating symptoms of ADHD, then therapy may be the perfect solution for your child. Therapy helps children with ADHD learn those essential life skills that don't come so easily to them, such as organization, time management, and social behavior. A therapist will also work with your child to discover strategies and methods that enhance their listening and focus, helping them improve in school and social settings and setting them up for a bright future.

Personally, one of my favorite aspects of therapy for children with ADHD is that it gives them an outlet for those tricky and intense emotions—all of those feelings that usually lead to huge outbursts and tantrums. A therapist serves as an additional support system for your child, one who can teach them how to convert feelings of anger and anxiety into productive and positive thoughts and actions.

Another added benefit is that it can be combined with medicine, providing your child with two different types of care. Remember that the duration of therapy entirely depends on your child's goals. Typically, a therapist will suggest one weekly session for a few months, creating a consistent and reliable regimen. During this time, your child will work on their ADHD by completing activities and sharing their ideas. They may ease anxiety with mindful meditation for one week while learning listening skills the following.

Here's a more in-depth description of what happens in ADHD therapy:

- **Talking and Listening:** A therapist will teach your child how to talk about complex emotions such as anxiety and stress. They'll learn how to identify and express them

through words instead of hurtful actions. This also shows them the value of listening and talking to others.
- **Playing with a Purpose:** Usually, players play games that teach valuable life lessons, such as waiting to take turns, following instructions, or trying again rather than giving up. This time will also be used to show your child how to organize, plan, and even put things away.
- **Doing Activities That Teach Lessons:** A therapist will direct a significant portion of their time to improving essential life skills such as organizing schoolwork, studying, and understanding others and their emotions.
- **Practicing New Skills:** Life can present many tricky situations that are difficult to manage, even for kids. So, a therapist helps your child build a toolkit of self-soothing strategies for these situations, for example, mindfulness meditations for anxiety-provoking moments or breathing exercises in times of frustration.

If the following activities sound like something that may benefit your child, then you might want to check out the following two types of ADHD therapy:

- **Cognitive Behavioral Therapy (CBT):** CBT is debatably the best therapy for children with ADHD. It focuses directly on solving daily struggles like procrastination, poor organization, planning, and time management. It's perfect for any child looking to ditch negative behavior and reframe their emotions and actions in a more positive light.
- **Dialectal Behavioral Therapy:** If your child experiences behavioral struggles, such as emotional regulation, distress tolerance, and inattentive symptoms, dialectal behavioral therapy offers a great solution. This therapy helps young

minds overcome challenging feelings and emotional symptoms of ADHD through meditative practices and simple yet effective strategies.

As you can see, therapy is super beneficial for kids, tweens, teens, and even adults. If you're unsure if it's the correct treatment for your child, consider chatting with a local practitioner. Perhaps asking them a few questions and having a session or two with you present will give you a better perspective on what treatment is right for your family dynamic.

Medication

Medication is one of those topics that can spark a lot of concern in us parents; I can't be the only one who considered the plethora of side effects and possible pitfalls of ADHD medication and thought, "Is this really worth it?"

The answer to this question would be yes; it is worth it. While medication can feel daunting, today's advancement in technology and pharmaceuticals has allowed us to have an array of options to try. Plus, each child's experience with medication is completely different. All it requires is a little trial and error to see which one is most suitable for your child's mental and physical well-being. If you are able to find a medication that suits your specific needs and enhances your child's school life, social interactions, and emotional distress, the benefits truly do pay off.

Typically, medication is prescribed to ease the impact and severity of your child's ADHD symptoms, especially the ones that influence their daily life, such as poor attention or impulsivity. Depending on the medication, it'll be taken one to two times a day by mouth. Some doctors may even offer a liquid form or patch that can be placed on the arm.

So, what type of medication can a child with ADHD be prescribed? Let's take a look:

- **Stimulants:** This medication works as soon as it is taken and can either be short-acting, lasting three to six hours, or long-acting, lasting ten to twelve hours. Common stimulant medications include methylphenidate, like Ritalin, Concerta, Focalin, and Daytrana, and amphetamines, such as Adderall, Dexedrine, and Vyvanse.
- **Non-stimulants:** This medication is often prescribed if stimulants aren't compatible with the child. A doctor will also want to ensure that herbal remedies, over-the-counter medication, and supplements aren't being used. Non-stimulants include atomoxetine, clonidine, guanfacine, and viloxazine.

Bear in mind that the dosage and side effects will vary depending on the child. Your doctor will be there to help guide you through the process and continuously ensure that the prescribed medication is a good match for your child. As your child grows, expect the medication to fluctuate and change with them. Don't forget that it's also important to include them in this new stage of their life and check up on them occasionally.

THE ADVANTAGES

Before we conclude this chapter, it's only fair that we shed some much-needed love and light on the wonderful aspects of ADHD. After all, it's one of the best superpowers a person could have. In case you didn't realize it before, your child possesses an array of qualities that benefit their life in so many aspects. Just take a look for yourself:

- **Creativity:** While you may be wondering if your child will turn into this generation's Picasso, they're busy whipping up their next exciting adventure. And no, this doesn't mean they just booked a direct flight to Greece. Children with ADHD are incredibly creative; they enjoy the simplest activities as their minds burst with new ideas and notions on how they'll play out. Even when the task at hand is a bit trickier than usual, they're open to thinking outside the box and coming up with creative solutions. Not to mention, they are naturally talented at instruments, art, dance, sports, and acting!
- **Hyperfocus:** When your child finds an activity they enjoy, they pour their heart and soul into it. Seriously, when hyperfocused mode is switched on, they become extremely dedicated and committed, so much so that you may even find it difficult to direct their attention to other tasks. The key is to find your child's special talent and enjoy the process of trying out every hobby imaginable. Sooner or later, they'll find their true calling, creating a future full of potential, fulfillment, and contentment!
- **Risk Tolerance:** Teens, tweens, and children with ADHD truly define what it means to be a risk-taker. From battling a million and one daily challenges to constantly pushing themselves to try new hobbies, meet new people, and set out on new adventures, they're beyond brave.
- **High Energy:** While all children with ADHD may not have hyperactive symptoms, most are incredibly energetic. If you want to go swimming in the morning, meet up with friends in the afternoon, and finish the day with a hike, they're the people to call. No one portrays positivity and radiant energy better than them!

- **Resilience:** Whether you have a teen, tween, or little one with ADHD, chances are they face a handful of obstacles every day. Yet they wake up every morning ready to tackle anything that enters their path. When they get knocked down, they get straight back up, even with a smile on their face. If anything, our little one motivates us to be more resilient, whether they have ADHD or not!
- **Spontaneity and Courage:** While little ones with ADHD thrive with schedules and routines, they'd be happy to ditch them and hit up the next adventure within seconds. While most would fear the unknown and shy away from opportunity and growth, kids with ADHD revel in it. They're spontaneous and courageous, and they dare to be bold at any chance that they get!

See, I told you ADHD was a superpower! Isn't your little one lucky?

SUMMARY

Types of ADHD	1. Inattentive. 2. Hyperactive-Impulsive. 3. Combined.
Misconceptions about ADHD	• Only boys can have ADHD. • ADHD is the result of poor parenting. • ADHD is a childhood issue and will go away.
Assessment Guidelines for ADHD Diagnosis	• Symptoms manifest in two or more settings, like home, school, and social environments, resulting in some level of impairment. • For children aged four to seventeen, a minimum of six symptoms should be discernible. • For individuals aged seventeen and above, a minimum of five symptoms should be discernible.

	• Symptoms significantly hinder your child's functioning in various daily activities, including academics, family and peer relationships, and group engagements like sports. • The onset of symptoms predates the age of twelve, though they may not be recognized as ADHD symptoms until later. • Symptoms persist for over six months.
ADHD Therapies	• Cognitive behavioral therapy (CBT). • Dialectal behavioral therapy.
ADHD Medications	• Stimulant. • Non-stimulant.
Advantages of ADHD	• Creativity. • Hyperfocus. • Risk tolerance. • High energy. • Resilience. • Spontaneity and courage.

JOURNALING FOR SELF-REFLECTION

Well done for completing the first chapter in this new phase of parenting; I can see where your child gets their unwavering bravery, courage, and strength from. Before we begin Chapter 2, let's take a moment to unwind and reflect by following along with the journaling prompts below:

1. What are your top three strengths, and how do they impact your family?
2. What are your three weaknesses, and how do they impact your family?
3. What did your child do today that was new in their development and growth? How did this impact you?
4. Who or what inspires you to strive to be a better parent?
5. What are your current parenting goals?

MUST-HAVE PARENTING SKILLS

> *Kids won't "outgrow" ADHD. They will learn to cope with it and accommodate it with a lot of hard work on their part and my part.*
>
> — H.C.

The reality of ADHD is that it can't be outgrown; it's a neurodevelopmental condition ingrained in your child, whether you like it or not. Hence, it makes perfect sense that you not only learn to love ADHD but also adapt a variety of essential parenting skills that will provide you and your child with the support and guidance needed to thrive. ADHD doesn't have to be chaotic, stressful, or feared. It can be empowering, whimsical, joyful, and a true blessing.

So, what are we waiting for? Let's delve into this chapter so you can learn fundamental skills for parenting a child with ADHD!

CHALLENGES OF PARENTING A CHILD WITH ADHD

Before we begin unpacking the secret solutions to parenting a child with ADHD, we must understand the full scope of how challenging it can be. Educating yourself as a parent goes beyond looking at the positive side. It involves being realistic and honest about the situation at hand. This is incredibly important if you have a child with ADHD, as there are often many challenges involved, day in and day out. You need to be able to identify the struggle, understand what measures should be taken, and know if you can fight this battle on your own or with the help of others. Let's take a look at the most common challenges of parenting a child with ADHD:

- **Marital Stress:** According to a study conducted by Wymbs et al. (2008), roughly 23 percent of married parents to a child with ADHD get divorced. On the other hand, parents with neurotypical children were only 12 percent likely to get a divorce. Bear in mind THAT this statistic doesn't mean you and your partner are destined to separate. It signifies that a lot of additional stress is placed on parents of children with ADHD, making it super important that you nurture your marital relationship. Spending time together, learning healthy communication, and making decisions about your child's behavior as a team will put this static to shame!
- **Isolation:** When you're a parent to a child with ADHD, it can feel as if you're the only one experiencing the ups and downs of neurodivergence. The seemingly never-ending list of daily challenges can get the best of your mental health, leaving you with feelings of anxiety, stress, and loneliness. Joining online forums, finding a support group, and speaking to a mental health professional can help

alleviate these feelings. Prioritizing your mental well-being is essential for any parent.
- **Boredom:** We all know that children with ADHD are quick to boredom, but what about you? While being a parent truly is a blessing, no one enjoys repeating instructions twelve times or following the same rules and schedules every single day. As great as consistency is, it gets boring. The best way to combat the boredom without packing your bags for a weekend trip to Ibiza is by taking 10–15 minutes to do something completely unrelated to your child. Whether it's calling up a friend to talk about the latest celeb gossip or going for a walk with your favorite tunes playing, take some time to do something you enjoy.
- **Feelings of Guilt:** Ugh, the dreaded shame, blame, and guilt that parents are plagued with. As parents, there truly are no limits as to what you feel guilty about. Whether it's accidentally losing your patience or switching your ears off when your child is telling you something, that pesky feeling always finds a way to pop up. It's important that we understand that these feelings are normal and come with parenting a child with ADHD. When feelings of shame, blame, or guilt arise, acknowledge them, accept them, and move on.
- **Consistency in Discipline:** Disciplining any child is challenging. However, when the child in question has ADHD, it suddenly becomes ten times harder. Children with ADHD find it particularly difficult to maintain consistent rules as they struggle to remember expectations. This can be super stressful for you as a parent, as it can create issues at school, in social settings, and at home.

- **Academic Success:** It's no secret that children with ADHD often struggle with completing homework, learning at school, and even making friends. This combination of challenges can present a whirlwind of stress and overwhelm, as it's often completely out of your hands. The best way to support your child's academic success is by discovering their unique needs and approaching them with a solution-oriented mindset.
- **Social Skills:** If you ever want to test your patience as a parent, you should try teaching your child with ADHD social skills. These bundles of joy often find it difficult to identify social cues and understand body language. Not to mention that regulating their emotions can feel borderline impossible.

Now that you have a greater idea of the struggles of parenting a child with ADHD, let it empower you. Feeling overwhelmed, stressed, and anxious is easily done, but that won't serve you in your journey toward becoming a supportive and strong parent. You're ready to face any challenge life offers; take pride in that. To help boost your confidence and prepare you even further, consider using the following tips to navigate parenting a child with ADHD:

- **Spend time learning about your child's unique challenges.** Just because ADHD is a common disorder doesn't mean it is the same for everyone. Each individual with ADHD has their own experience. This is why it is so important that you work with your child to understand what their symptoms look like and how this affects their daily life.
- **Understand co-occurring conditions.** Children with ADHD may also have a co-occurring condition, such as anxiety, depression, or a learning disability. These

disorders can make it more difficult to treat ADHD and, once again, require a tailored approach. If you believe your child may have a co-occurring condition, speaking with a medical professional is always best.

- **Find the right treatment for your child.** More often than not, your child will receive their diagnosis, and your parental brain will instantly jump to "Oh no, my child needs to take medication!" While there is nothing wrong with traditional medicine, there exists a plethora of holistic remedies for symptoms of ADHD. From herbal concoctions to behavioral therapy and social training, it's important you find the right treatment for your child.
- **Praise your child when they do something well.** Research has uncovered that praise is more important for neurodivergent children than it is for neurotypical children (Fosco et al. 2015). Positive reinforcement involves encouraging your child to repeat positive behavior through verbal and physical rewards. Picture it as sunlight to a plant; in order for the sapling to blossom into a tree, it needs the warmth and care of the sun. If you want your child to meet positive expectations, you must encourage them.
- **Prepare your child for transitions.** Switching video games off, finishing up an activity, or turning off a show can lead to bargaining, refusal, and even huge tantrums. Transitioning from one activity to another can create a lot of resistance in your child, especially if they enjoy whatever they are doing. To avoid meltdowns and tantrums, ensure your child is aware of the upcoming transition. This can be done by setting a timer with a countdown displayed, reading through your child's schedule with them, and praising them for seamless

transitions. You'll be back to watching your favorite shows before you know it!

Creating and enforcing consistent rules and expectations will slowly but surely improve your child's behavior. Before you've even realized it, your stress levels will have improved, and those pesky feelings of shame, blame, and guilt will have disappeared!

ADJUSTING PARENTING STYLE

Parenting is an incredibly rewarding and magnificent journey that comes with unpredictable twists and turns as well as a million and one hurdles. When these precious little angles are born, you experience a mix of emotions: joy, awe, excitement, overwhelm, and exhaustion. You do everything you can to care and provide for them while slowly accepting that your life has changed forever. Each day that passes can feel like a blessing but also a nightmare; you're desperate for a full night's sleep, yet the thought of missing a moment with your child evokes feelings of sadness and regret. You thought it would get easier with time, that once they grew, became independent, and discovered their own way in life, parental pressure would simply drift away. But it doesn't; whether your child has ADHD or not, and no matter their age, they will always need you and look to you for guidance.

So, this only leaves us with one option: to become awesome parents who are willing and committed to growing with our children and learning, adapting, and improving with every chance we get. There is no shame in admitting that parenting isn't easy or that you've made mistakes and could have been better. Showing up each and every day, prepared to make a positive impact on your child's life, is what counts. With this being said, let's take a look at a few parenting styles and how they affect a child with ADHD:

- **Authoritarian Parenting:** Authoritarian parenting takes a more strict and demanding approach, where punishment is often used to teach right from wrong. While it's good to expect the best from your child, harsh discipline can intensify symptoms of ADHD and lead to a cycle of harmful, repetitive behavior. Acting cold and strict toward your child can cause resentment and rebellious behavior. Not to mention that constant criticism would make anyone feel inadequate and discouraged from trying new things and setting new goals. This parenting style is not recommended and should be replaced with a more empathetic approach.
- **Permissive Parenting:** No one enjoys confrontation, but when you avoid it too much, you become lenient and indulgent and lack healthy boundaries for your child. Poor parenting structure leads to inconsistent rules. This could cause your child issues with maintaining healthy relationships and establishing boundaries. Without clear expectations, your child may lack direction and miss opportunities for growth. Additionally, when they meet an authoritative figure, such as a teacher or employer with high expectations, they may rebel, lack respect for them, and struggle to follow simple rules or instructions. While you may be tempted to let your child learn for themselves, clear expectations and healthy boundaries are paramount for a child with ADHD.
- **Uninvolved Parenting:** Life can be tough, especially when you have a mountain of personal issues, financial problems, and stress to deal with. However, detaching yourself from your child and becoming unresponsive can be extremely damaging. Undoubtedly, feeling unloved and lacking emotional support will leave a child with a poor sense of self-worth. This will be reflected in the actions

they take as an adult as well as their academics. Keep in mind that children with ADHD thrive in a loving and supportive environment, so when these needs aren't met, it intensifies symptoms and may lead to depression. This parenting style is not recommended; your child needs support and care to navigate the ups and downs of ADHD.

- **Authoritative Parenting:** Think of authoritative parenting as the go-to approach; it's warm, loving, and attentive to your child's needs while setting clear and consistent boundaries, expectations, and routines. The child follows a scheduled routine that isn't overwhelming and is praised and rewarded for good behavior. They're also given a bundle of support, empathy, and understanding, effectively nurturing a strong relationship between you and your child. As a result, you're able to build trust and healthy communication and create an environment that embraces growth and change.

No parent is perfect; you can read every book, implement every strategy, and still make a few hiccups. But when you begin noticing your mistakes, accepting them, and improving yourself, you'll know you're on the right path. Let's take a look at my top six tips and tricks for parenting a child with ADHD:

- **Establish routines.** While you may have never guessed it, routines and schedules are the backbones for children with ADHD. Those little ones are messy, chaotic, unorganized, and pretty bad with time, but when it comes to consistent, healthy routines, they succeed like no one else. We'll look closer at establishing routines to reduce stress and increase productivity later.

- **Set clear expectations.** Children with ADHD need rules and guidelines to follow; otherwise, they can feel quite confused and without a sense of direction. The best way to set expectations is through visualization. For instance, if you expect your child to be kind and compassionate, you must explain to them what this means and show them how they can execute this with their siblings or toward you, and then perhaps a poster on a wall will help instill consistency. Your child has to understand the consequences of their actions and behavior.
- **Give positive reinforcement.** Positive reinforcement involves rewarding your child when they exhibit good behavior, such as kindness. When you notice them acting and behaving positively or meeting your expectations, encourage them to repeat the behavior through positive affirmations and a little reward. This can look like, "Well done for being so kind to your brother! Would you like to go to the park for ice cream?" or "You did so well on your test today! Would you like to go watch that new movie now?"
- **Offer choices.** As we know, setting clear and consistent boundaries is super important. Offering choices within this boundary empowers your child and also improves their decision-making skills. For example, if you want them to be more active in chores around the house, perhaps ask them if they'd like to wipe the counter each night or pick up laundry from around the house. This way, they feel included and that their opinions matter.
- **Be patient and flexible.** As much as we wish healthy habits could be learned overnight and new routines could be implemented easily, it will take a lot of flexibility and patience as your child learns and adapts. It may take weeks

or months to see progress in their behavior and actions. Adjust as needed, and be patient.
- **Seek support.** Connecting with other parents, support groups, and professionals will allow you peace of mind, guidance, and even helpful resources. Showing up for your child also means showing up for yourself; if you need an extra shoulder to lean on, always reach out to a trusted friend, partner, or licensed professional.

Drawing the line between discipline and patience, routine and flexibility, and neurodivergence and neurotypicality can sometimes feel impossible. It's important to know that you're not alone in this journey. There are parents in the same position, facing the same battles, and combating identical challenges of ADHD. There is always hope, no matter how lonely or difficult parenting can feel. It's remarkable that you've cracked open this book and gotten this far. Keep going; you're doing amazing!

MUST-HAVE PARENTING SKILLS

There truly is no guide to parenting; we're bound to mess up and make a few mistakes along the way—that's just how life goes. However, little did you know that three super simple parenting skills hold the power to revolutionize your family dynamic. Whether you have a child with ADHD or not, consistency, patience, and empathy are must-have skills for any parent!

Consistency

In those moments where you feel nothing will ever improve your child's symptoms of ADHD, it's probably because you've forgotten to implement simple yet effective strategies such as consistency. You get stuck and overwhelmed by that feeling of defeat and exhaustion, ultimately clogging your brain and falling out of those healthy habits.

Consistent parenting involves having the same consequences for the same behavior; there are no fluctuations or changes depending on your mood or the circumstances. Time and time again, you demonstrate to your child that a certain behavior results in a particular consequence, whether that's positive or negative.

Consistency is ideal for children with ADHD, as they struggle immensely to remember rules and think about the consequences of their actions. Learning from experience will allow them to understand how their actions affect themselves and others. It requires repetition, time, and patience, but the benefits of consistency truly do pay off. Over time, your child will create their own little rule book, where they follow the guidelines to implement their new positive behavior at school, in social settings, and at home.

As a parent to a child with ADHD, you must prioritize consistency. If not, you may end up tired and drained by a repetitive routine of negative behavior. For instance, imagine you allow your nine-year-old child with ADHD to stay awake past 10 p.m. to watch a football match. A few days later, a basketball tournament is playing on the TV past 10 p.m., and you refuse and send your child to bed. This is inconsistent parenting; it may appear harmless, but to your ADHD child, it's confusing as to why you make one exception to the rule and not another. This lack of clarity becomes stressful and overwhelming for your child, leading to persuasive behavior, bargaining, and, ultimately, the dreaded tantrum.

As a parent, one of your jobs is to provide a clear and concise rulebook for your child that is easy to implement and understand. This can be done by following the five steps of consistent parenting:

- **Step One:** The first call of action is gathering the entire family in one room with a pen and paper. You'll need to create a simple rulebook that each member understands. You can even ask your kids what a fair consequence for not following a particular rule should be. For example, rule #1 may include placing all dirty laundry items into the hamper by 6 p.m. every day. The consequence may be folding the dry laundry or helping with the dishes. Remember that the rules and consequences should be age-appropriate for each child.
- **Step Two:** Identify three problematic areas, such as TV time, homework, or compassion, and work through clear solutions and consequences with your children. These three areas will be your main focus moving forward.
- **Step Three:** After the meeting, talk with your parenting partner or analyze the list alone. Be honest, and ask yourself if you are genuinely capable of maintaining each rule and consequence. You and your partner should be on the same page, without any doubt. If necessary, make changes to the list.
- **Step Four:** After you and your partner have taken a day or two to consider the new rulebook, call for another family meeting with your children. Go over each and every rule, asking your children to repeat and explain them back to you. This way, you'll be able to clarify any misunderstandings and ensure they "get" the rules. Don't forget to place the new rulebook in a visible spot where everyone can see it!
- **Step Five:** Lastly, you will need to organize a set time and day each week for family meetings. Over the next three months, as a team, you will need to monitor progress and evaluate your children's behavior, praising them for

everything they've done well and reviewing those hard-to-follow rules.

By following these five steps, you'll be able to sit back and watch your child change their behavior for the better and gradually meet your expectations.

Empathy

Explosive outbursts, temper fits, and tantrums over the simplest of situations are common occurrences in ADHD households. As a parent, how you react to emotional chaos is key to your child's emotional growth. Simply taking a step back and a deep breath may make a world of difference to how your child portrays and expresses their feelings.

Children with ADHD experience big emotions that are hard to manage. This is because they have emotional dysregulation, where their emotional response is poorly regulated and typically expressed in a manner that does not fit the situation at hand, for example, crying and screaming over turning the TV off. In this situation, it's essential that you demonstrate empathy by acknowledging their feelings and helping them find a solution, such as, "I understand you're really upset about turning the TV off, but it's time for you to go to bed. How about we take a minute to sit on the sofa and calm down, and then you go to bed?"

Typically, our immediate reaction to negative behavior like name-calling, hitting, and yelling is to spew out a million and one punishments and consequences. But, for a child with ADHD, being sent to their bedroom and confiscating toys and electronics accomplishes nothing. In fact, it can even escalate the situation and intensify their emotions.

Acting with empathy offers your child a sense of companionship through these challenging emotions. Discussing and acknowledging their feelings validates their experiences, helping them to identify and understand their emotions. Over time, your child will learn to name their feelings and discover effective ways to self-soothe. This is helpful for moments when you won't be by their side, like at school, social settings, or clubs. So, how can you become a more empathetic parent? Try implementing the following points:

- **Label your child's emotional state before you respond.** Labeling your child's emotional state will automatically trigger empathy as you consider how they're feeling and what they are currently experiencing. It may sound something like, "I see you're feeling sad right now. Is there anything I can do to help?"
- **Practice self-compassion.** Compassion starts within; this may mean hitting the pause button and taking some time out to pamper yourself. Simply reconnecting with activities you enjoy, engaging in some much-needed self-care, and journaling can reframe your state of mind into a more compassionate and caring head space.
- **Empathize.** It's important to remember that your child's feelings are real and valid. We often get caught up in how "dramatic" or "intense" an ADHD child's emotions are without considering how difficult they must be to manage or experience. As a parent, it is your job to recognize those feelings and help your little one work through them in the best way possible.
- **Contextualize your child's feelings in their developmental process.** No one is asking you to be a superhero here; your child may just need to save themselves in this situation. When your child is with you,

at home, and in a safe and supportive environment, this is the perfect time for them to learn how to come out on the other side. While supporting them, allow your child to feel their emotions and work through them by moving on to a new activity, talking, or reframing their mindset.

Patience

Children are notoriously messy, chaotic, and even accident-prone. However, hyperactivity, impulsivity, inattention, and nearly every other symptom of ADHD can really put your patience to the test.

Maintaining patience is crucial if you want to build a loving, supportive, and secure environment. Modeling positive behavior will not only build healthy communication between you and your child but also boost their self-esteem. Think about it: Little ones with ADHD are commonly put down for being too loud, disruptive, and busy. Having patience and showing them some empathy shows them that their ADHD isn't a negative thing, no matter how challenging it can be. Not to mention that learning the art of patience will also help you to alleviate some of that unnecessary stress!

Consider implementing the following tips to improve your patience with a child diagnosed with ADHD:

- **Learn strategies for regulating your own emotions.** Caring for any child can be emotionally and physically taxing. Managing those feelings of stress, overwhelm, and frustration can become even more difficult when exhaustion is thrown into the mix. While I'd like to recommend a full night's sleep, I know this isn't always possible. The next best thing is performing those simple yet important self-care rituals, practicing mindfulness, and

adopting coping strategies that help you get through those difficult days as easily as possible.
- **Know it is not your child's fault.** Remember, ADHD is a neurodevelopmental condition involving differences in brain functioning, chemicals, and structure. They're not acting out or behaving naughtily; they're simply being themselves. Rather than acting with blame, take a positive, empathetic, and encouraging approach.
- **Don't compare yourself to other parents you know.** Each child and family situation is different, and comparing yourself to others can make you feel inadequate or overwhelmed. Instead, focus on your own strengths and challenges. Trust your instincts, prioritize what works best for your family, and remember that there's no one right way to parent!

JOURNALING FOR SELF-REFLECTION

Before we conclude this chapter, let's take a moment to delve a bit deeper. Below, you'll find prompts designed to guide you through a journey of introspection and understanding:

1. What brings you a sense of tranquility?
2. What empowers you?
3. How do you establish limits to prevent taking on others' emotions and stress?
4. How do you grant yourself forgiveness after making a mistake?
5. How do you take time and prioritize your own needs?

OVERCOME BEHAVIORAL CHALLENGES

> *The hardest thing about ADHD is that it's "invisible" to outsiders. People just assume that we are not being good parents and that our child is a brat, when they don't have an idea how exhausted we truly are.*
>
> — S.C.

Parenting a child with ADHD involves more than what meets the eye. You see, others often mistake hyperactivity for naughtiness; impulsivity is labeled as bratty or rude, while poor attention skills are mistaken for stupidity. At times, parenting truly sucks, but only because no one else can see the beauty of ADHD. Our child is compassionate, enthusiastic, and creative. Our little one has more passion and power to live their life than most adults do. They can be one of the smartest kids in the room, but their talent hides behind the shadows and needs a little helping hand to be revealed. Others don't see the time, dedication, and effort it takes to repeat instructions ten times in a row, correct behaviors time and time again, and work on essential life skills that don't come easily. They can't see the love, support, and understanding that it takes to raise a child with superpowers.

WHAT TRIGGERS CHALLENGING BEHAVIORS?

In today's society, it's common to hear people use the word "trigger." You may have even heard your friend or partner say, "Ugh, please stop talking; you're triggering me," as you accidentally evoked negative emotions, a bad memory, or even trauma. Don't worry; we've all done this once or twice by mistake. But were you aware that children with ADHD also have their own list of triggers? Let's take a closer look.

A behavioral trigger is an action or situation that creates a negative emotion and response; it's more than being uncomfortable or upset. A trigger can impair your child's judgment and lead to actions and behaviors that they wouldn't typically display, such as outbursts and tantrums. Below, you'll find a list of the six most common behavioral triggers of children with ADHD:

- **Sleep Deprivation:** A poor night's sleep could ruin anyone's day, but for a child with ADHD, it can also intensify their symptoms. According to Wajszilber et al. (2018), 50 percent of individuals diagnosed with ADHD experience disrupted sleep, which can worsen symptoms like inattention, hyperactivity, forgetfulness, drowsiness, poor impulse control, and careless mistakes. This suggests that getting your child to bed on time is more important than ever, as the number of hours they sleep greatly impacts their emotions and behavior.
- **Stress:** Stress is one of those things that you simply can't avoid, even if you're a child. As you may know, living with ADHD can cause heaps of stress. The issue with this is that

stress can also magnify the symptoms of ADHD, fueling a cycle of undesirable behavior and intense emotions.
- **Certain Foods and Additives:** We all know that sugar and caffeine can set little ones off in a spiral of chaos. However, additives have also been found to aggravate symptoms of ADHD. A study conducted by Arnold et al. (2012) discovered a direct link between food coloring and symptoms of ADHD like hyperactivity and inattention. This could suggest that artificial foods and additives impact your child's behavior and emotions.
- **Overstimulation:** Think of overstimulation as a sensory overload where smells, sensations, tastes, and sounds become overbearing. As a result, it can make it really challenging for your child to concentrate and process what's happening around them. For instance, an itchy sweater, bright lights, or a stinky cafeteria can make them irritated and lose concentration. While overstimulation may seem minor, without effective management strategies, avoiding it simply won't work and will worsen behavioral issues.
- **Technology:** iPads, TVs, and phones are typically harmless, right? Yet switching them off or removing them nearly always leads to temper tantrums, crying fits, or poor concentration. This is because technology stimulates the mind and intensifies symptoms of ADHD. Bright screens, flashing lights, and excessive noise lead to pent-up energy and a lack of bodily movement, which can even ruin their attention span in the long run. While there aren't any studies confirming that technology influences ADHD, it can definitely trigger those not-so-great symptoms.

Bear in mind that everyone's triggers can vary and be completely different depending on their own experience with ADHD. The trick is to have a keen eye and pay close attention to your child's behavior. Sometimes, watching and listening to your child is the best thing you can do. Whether your child is completing their chores, talking with friends, or playing, pay extra attention to their behavioral patterns. For example, if they're playing with friends in the park but suddenly get hot and frustrated, it may be time to consider a sensory overload. If your teen gets sassy and rude when it's time to complete their homework, perhaps they're stressed. Keep your eyes and ears open as you apply a magnifying glass to every situation where a rapid behavioral change occurs. Soon enough, you'll connect the dots and uncover a few hidden triggers!

It's also important to remember that your child's, tween's, or teen's perception may be completely different from yours. As parents, we always want to help our little ones feel better, but we may accidentally skip past uncovering what actually happened. Just because you witnessed it doesn't mean you know the full scope. So, even when you think you know the full story, sit down with your child and take some time to understand their perspective. Who knows? You may just uncover a whole new story!

Understanding your child's triggers will help you both tremendously. You'll be able to provide them with the correct resources to improve their self-awareness and regulate their emotions while they practice fundamental self-management skills. As time passes, your little one will become more aware of their feelings and triggers, contributing to a positive outlook and enhancing their critical thinking. The benefits practically unfold all by themselves!

All that's left is to set your child on the right path with these five tips and tricks that will boost their self-awareness:

- **With younger kids, talk about feelings.** Triggers and feelings are best friends; they go hand in hand, making it super important that your child has a good understanding of emotions. Try sitting down with your little one and talking about different kinds of feelings. Ask them what makes them feel happy, angry, and sad. You want your child to have a solid foundation, as this will allow them to identify their feelings and not excuse poor behavior.
- **Connect the dots for them.** Whether your child is two or twenty, they may need a little help connecting the dots. A parental perspective can be really helpful when it comes to understanding how and what your child is feeling. Big emotions can be complex and confusing, no matter the age. Consider using simple and gentle language, such as "Whenever _____ happens, you seem _____."
- **Talk about the signs.** As we discussed before, being triggered involves more than feeling upset. It also comes with many physical symptoms, such as a rapid heartbeat, sweating, cold hands, tensed muscles, shortness of breath, and flushed cheeks. Discussing these physical signs and symptoms will allow your child to gain a better understanding of what's happening in their body; it may even reduce anxiety and stress!
- **Use cues.** Cueing is an awesome behavioral management technique that allows you to practice healthy communication with your child in moments of high stress and anxiety. Once you and your child have established a particular trigger, make a simple hand signal or phrase that serves as an alert to your child when said trigger arises. Whether in a social situation or at home, you and your child can communicate effectively with minimal stress and practice adequate emotional regulation tools.

- **Check in.** If you notice that your child can't self-soothe and regulate their emotions after being triggered, it may be time for you to check in and help them out. Here, you will need to remind your child of the behavior they're displaying and its possible consequences.

HYPERACTIVITY AND IMPULSIVITY

A hyperactive and impulsive child defines energy better than anyone; seriously, they're productive bundles of joy. However, when this energy isn't managed effectively or directed into a positive outlet, it can lead to a variety of disruptive symptoms. For example, your child may struggle with sitting still, resisting urges to tap their hands or feet, and squirming in their seat. They may be jumping around, climbing obstacles you didn't know were climbable, and finding it difficult to do any activity quietly. Not to mention that making and managing friends can feel virtually impossible as they blurt out their thoughts, interrupt others, and struggle to wait for their turn.

It's normal for children to have high energy and short attention spans; hyperactivity goes beyond this. Your child will appear to be constantly on the go, and these symptoms can even be detrimental to their well-being. Think about it: Climbing and risky behavior can lead to unintentional injuries like burns, falls, and fractures, ultimately posing a threat to their physical well-being. As they grow older, this risky behavior can manifest in different aspects of their lives, such as high-risk substances and illegal activity. Unmanaged hyperactivity and impulsivity can also lead to relationship struggles and interpersonal violence.

While the disadvantages of hyperactivity and impulsivity can feel extreme and like distant issues, providing your child with effective strategies that help them successfully manage their symptoms of

ADHD will set them up for a bright future. Below, you'll find my top strategies for managing hyperactivity and impulsivity in children with ADHD:

- **Be Explicit:** In our head, we have a detailed picture of how we want our children to behave; whether it's kind, compassionate, or daring, we all have a list of qualities that we're eager to see in them. When they act contrary to this idealized list, we tend to lash out and offer a handful of consequences without considering if they even knew about expectations in the first place. Sit down with your child and explain the difference between positive and negative behavior. Then, tell them your expectations; you can even create a cool poster with your child!
- **Consistent Follow-Through:** Once your child understands your expectations, ensure you and any parental figure at home are consistent with the consequences. If not, you run the risk of the behavior being repeated. This is especially important for hyperactive, impulsive children, who must understand that their actions are within their control. Every urge and impulse should not be listened to; there is a clear difference between right and wrong.
- **Swift Follow-Throughs:** Remember, children with ADHD have poor memory skills, meaning a delayed punishment may lead to confusion and a lack of significance. Both positive and negative consequences should be followed through as soon as possible. It may help to create a big list of rewards and consequences for typical hyperactive-impulsive behavioral issues.
- **Be a Good Role Model:** Your child looks up to you; as their role model, it's your responsibility to show them right from wrong through your words and actions. For

instance, if you lose your temper due to stress, you demonstrate that this behavior is acceptable and allow them to mirror this behavior at school or with friends. The idea is that you represent the person you want your child to grow up to be, set the example, and watch them follow!

One of the more challenging sides to ADHD is impulsivity, where every itch has to be scratched. If your child struggles to manage their impulses, consider teaching them the following impulse control techniques:

- **Ask your child to repeat directions.** It's no secret that most of what we say goes in one ear and out the other, which may be one of the reasons your child is acting impulsively. To help them stay on track, get your child to repeat instructions back to you. Whether it's completing their homework or cleaning their room, they should be able to explain what expectations and instructions you've outlined for them. Remember to keep directions simple and easy to follow; you can even write them down if you feel it's needed.
- **Teach problem-solving skills.** Problem-solving skills don't come easily to children with ADHD, so it's super important to give them a helping hand. Show your child that there is more than one way to solve an issue. Try grabbing a pen and paper and bullet point five ways to solve a math problem or fix a broken picture frame. Get your child to join the brainstorming session and welcome any creative ideas. Practicing problem-solving skills will demonstrate how important it is to think before you act.

- **Play impulse control games.** No one said impulse control had to be boring. Board games, *Simon Says*, and *Red Light, Green Light* are simple yet enjoyable tools for practicing self-control.

And just like that, you've learned how to master hyperactivity and impulsivity. Now, you have all the tools necessary to help your child live a more productive lifestyle!

INATTENTIVENESS

Although hyperactivity is part of the ADHD name, it doesn't mean that all children with ADHD are hyperactive. Some children struggle more with inattentiveness, which mainly consists of poor attention skills. According to the NHS (2021), roughly two out of ten children experience difficulty concentrating and focusing rather than managing hyperactivity. These children typically experience the following symptoms of inattentiveness:

- Having a limited attention span and getting distracted easily.
- Making unintentional errors and mistakes, such as in school assignments.
- Seeming forgetful or frequently misplacing items.
- Struggling to stay focused on tasks that are boring or lengthy.
- Seeming unable to follow or execute instructions.
- Frequently switching between activities or tasks.
- Finding it challenging to organize tasks.

While poor attention skills may seem mild or meek, they can manifest in multiple areas of your child's life and cause substantial challenges, such as:

- **Poor academic performance:** There is more to life than good grades and an honor roll. However, academic achievement plays a significant role in your child's self-esteem, especially in those pivotal years of development. When a little one notices their grades aren't as high as their peers', it can leave them feeling left out, inadequate, and different. This is one of the reasons why it's so important to seek a diagnosis at a young age, or they may grow up to believe they are simply unintelligent, out of place, and insufficient. Depending on your child's career choices, academic success may also play a key role in financial stability and vocational fulfillment.
- **Unfortunate Labels Like "Slow Learners" or "Learning Disabled":** Firstly, it's important to recognize that ADHD isn't a learning disability, but it can make learning more difficult. This is because children with ADHD process information differently from others; their memory isn't so great, meaning visualization is crucial, and instructions often need to be repeated. Poor attention skills can also make focusing really challenging, meaning test results and exams don't always come back with stellar marks.
- **Undue Shame:** Building on our second point, mislabeling an ADHD child as a slow learner or disabled creates a sense of undue shame. They're just as capable as the person next to them, yet they're portrayed incorrectly, ultimately leaving them feeling alienated and neglected. Children with inattentive symptoms simply require a different toolkit than other kids, one that works with their ADHD brain rather than against it.
- **Indifference:** Inattentive symptoms often go unnoticed by doctors, teachers, and parents. This is because the child's struggle is internalized and rather hard to spot; teachers and parents may simply believe their child requires a tutor

or isn't working hard enough. In reality, they're facing an internal battle where their mind is running a million miles an hour, bombarded with thoughts and ideas as they struggle to focus on the task at hand. Trust me: Your child has considered speaking up. They've likely taken tests and attempted activities while questioning why everyone else can remain focused and they can't. A concoction of shame, inadequacy, and fear has isolated them in their struggle.

No one wants to see their child struggle in silence, nor should any child, tween, or teen feel alienated and neglected. Not to mention, the strategies for managing incentives are super simple and easy to implement. Within a few months, your child will be back on track, feeling confident and strong, and soaring through school. So, if you're ready to set your child on the path to success, consider implementing the following tips and tricks:

- **Make a to-do list.** The beauty of to-do lists is that they are so easy to make. With a piece of paper and a pen, simply write down lists of tasks, homework, or chores that your child needs to complete. This list should be easy to read and placed in a visible location so your child can read it.
- **Create bite-size projects.** Children with inattentive ADHD tend to get pretty overwhelmed with tasks as they struggle to organize and remember instructions. The best way to hack stress and overwhelm is by breaking down projects into bite-size chunks. For example, if you've asked your child to load the dishwasher, you'll need to break it down into simple steps, such as beginning by taking the dirty dishes and scraping leftover food into the trash can. Place the dirty dishes in the dishwasher. Repeat those two steps until the dishwasher is fully loaded, and add a cleaning tablet before pressing start. This may seem

longwinded, but as your child becomes more familiar with tackling projects, you'll be able to group certain details together, where cleaning the kitchen is broken down into loading the dishwasher, wiping the kitchen counters, and sweeping the floor.
- **Organize.** If you want your child to be organized, then, as their parent, you have to meet the same expectations. Remember, you're setting the example, so maintaining a tidy living environment will help them stay on track. Try to keep school clothes, books, materials, and toys all in their own spot; your child should know where to look if they need something. This allows your child to mirror the same behavior!
- **Cut down on distractions.** Turning off the TV, phone, iPad, and radio will help massively when it comes to minimizing distractions and enhancing focus.
- **Teach them self-monitoring.** Picture self-monitoring as simply increasing your child's self-awareness. It involves teaching your child about inattentiveness and making them aware that they have a tendency to drift off now and then. Be careful not to make this appear as a negative trait, and emphasize how it can even contribute to creativity and problem-solving.

Be mindful that organization, to-do lists, and self-monitoring will take a lot of time and practice. Take each day as it comes, and always treat your child's inattentive symptoms with compassion and understanding. Believe it or not, they want to be just as successful as you expect them to be!

TANTRUMS

Tantrums, outbursts, meltdowns, and hissy fits can be really difficult to manage, especially if they involve explosive behavior. In fact, aggressive outbursts are common in children with ADHD as they struggle to regulate emotions and control impulses. This means that hearing the word "later" or "no" can drastically take a turn for the worst and result in screaming, crying, and frustration. And while you may not want to admit it, these little angels can suddenly turn into your worst nightmare!

Whether your child has a tantrum at home or in public, they're never easy to handle. However, I do have a few tips that just might make it a bit easier for you to manage:

- **Find the trigger.** Understanding the root of the problem can help de-escalate a tantrum, something we parents all desire to do quickly. Ask yourself: Are they hungry, tired, or hurt? Could they be overstimulated?
- **Repeat the rules.** Children with ADHD have a hard time remembering rules and consequences they can't see. Repeating the expectations, rules, and consequences you previously established as a team will help them understand the behavior they're expected to model. In certain situations, you can also try giving them a moment or two to calm down and process the information. You may need to follow through with the consequences if the tantrum persists.
- **Take care of their needs.** Taking care of your child's needs doesn't mean that you are tolerating unacceptable behavior; you're simply caring for your child. Whether it's a hug, a calming conversation, or reassurance, always try your best to meet your child's needs.

- **Show the child how to behave.** Always remember that you are setting an example! If you want emotional outbursts to stop, then you must not display signs of anger or aggression in front of your child. You must model the behavior that you expect your child to follow. In heated situations, always remain calm, firm, and neutral.

Bear in mind that every child has tantrums, even the ones that are organized and get good grades; it's just a part of childhood. However, ADHD cannot be an excuse for aggressive behavior. Suppose your child frequently experiences emotional outbursts lasting more than 15 minutes that involve your child wrecking the entire house. In that case, it may be time to speak to a child psychologist or pediatrician for advice. Grabbing items and smashing them on the floor, hitting and slapping you, or, if they're older, spurring verbal abuse is simply unacceptable and not a characteristic of ADHD.

DISCIPLINE STRATEGIES

Let's face it: Your child faces unique challenges, all of which will involve trial and error. Their symptoms of ADHD will be triggered from time to time. They'll have outbursts and tantrums that drive them up the wall and shift their mood from happy to sad at the click of their fingers—all of which make parenting a beautiful yet challenging experience. These unique obstacles require different parenting strategies from those typically used for a neurotypical child.

Discipline is fundamental when it comes to managing impulsivity, improving focus, and controlling tantrums. This is because children with ADHD typically act before thinking, meaning that they do not consider the consequences of their actions. Not to mention that little ones with ADHD have super short attention spans, making homework, chores, and activities short-lasting. Discipline allows for a tailored approach to parenting, where you can positively teach your child right from wrong and direct them in a more productive headspace. You'll be able to nurture your child's growth, self-esteem, and independence with a simple but effective toolkit. Take a look for yourself:

- **Parents' Personal Discipline:** When your child is screaming in your ear, yanking on your arm, and crying profusely as if it's the end of the world, you can be tempted to yell back. However, this never really solves nor achieves anything apart from setting fear and anxiety in your child. To avoid unhealthy parenting patterns, you're going to need to become disciplined yourself. This means consistently approaching stressful situations with a calm and level-headed mentality. The best approach is always neutral.
- **Consistency and Routine:** Structure is essential for a healthy upbringing. According to the National Institute of Mental Health (2023), children thrive when regular schedules are set for bedtimes, homework, friends, and hobbies, as it helps regulate their energy and emotions. It also implies that aggressive outbursts are less likely to occur, preventing trouble before it even begins. Don't worry. We'll take a closer look at this in the following chapter!
- **Reinforcement of Positive Behaviors**: As heartbreaking as it is to watch your child cry, some tantrums must be ignored. If your child attempts to manipulate a situation, such as turning off the TV or completing homework, you must ignore their behavior. They will eventually get the message that manipulation doesn't work and that the TV

won't be turned back on. In addition to ignoring outbursts, you also need to be attentive to positive behavior. Quickly rewarding children for productive behaviors such as compassion, focus, and sharing will encourage them to repeat them.

CREATE YOUR REWARDS CHART

While I wish rewarding good behavior was as simple as saying "well done" and handing over a sticker, you need to consider a few things, such as selectivity, special circumstances, and even the method. Personally, I believe a point/token system is one of the easiest and most effective strategies for all age groups. A token system allows your children to earn points or tokens for completing goals, tasks, and chores. These tokens can be collected and then exchanged for rewards, such as a trip to the cinema or the park!

Keep in mind that you need to tell your children why they are being rewarded, as it may not be as obvious as you think. Being specific about praise and rewards will allow your children to repeat favorable behavior easily. Without clarity, your child will find it harder to regulate their emotions. For example, if your child cleans their bedroom, try saying something like, "Great job for cleaning your room!" You've highlighted the quality of the work and why they're being rewarded. You must also ensure not to praise trivial or minor accomplishments, such as putting a glass in the dishwasher. Your family should also agree on a point-and-reward system as a team so no one feels left out. Don't forget to ask your children to make a cool poster for the wall to help them visualize their behavioral goals and track their tokens!

JOURNALING FOR SELF-REFLECTION

As we conclude Chapter 3, mastering the art of discipline and overcoming behavioral challenges, let's take a moment to reflect on our journey with the following journaling prompts:

1. What are three specific areas in which you want to improve as a parent? Why are these areas important to you, and what steps can you take to work on them?
2. List some of your strengths as a parent and recent accomplishments you're proud of. How can you build on these strengths to continue growing?
3. Think about a time when you truly understood your child's feelings and perspective. What did you do to connect with them? How can you create more of these moments?
4. How do you define love?
5. Write about a person you admire. What qualities do you share with them?

BUILDING BLOCKS OF SUCCESS

> *Executive function challenges are often mistaken for disobedience, laziness, defiance, or apathy.*
>
> — CHRIS ZEIGLER DENDY, M.S.

When your child has ADHD, you come to realize how greatly the disorder is misunderstood; seriously, it's almost as if it hasn't been around since the early 1900s. Words like lazy, rude, and high maintenance are thrown around as if they don't carry any weight, leaving our little ones with a heavy burden on their shoulders. But here's the truth: Every child, regardless of their challenges, deserves to feel a sense of control and belonging. Children with ADHD are no exception. They have unique strengths and perspectives that can shine brilliantly when given the right support and understanding. So, let's tap into that light and harness their strengths!

ROUTINE AND STRUCTURE

Who would have thought that children with ADHD thrive with strict routines and schedules? While structure almost contradicts their fun and spontaneous personalities, ADHD is best managed when routines are implemented. Think of structure as the backbone of your child's day; it enables them to carry out their lives in an organized and predictable environment, meaning that all those chaotic symptoms and thoughts are far more contained. One study even found that structure helped children with ADHD regulate their emotions and behavior (Fiese B. 2002). Let's take a further look at how routine can be beneficial for our little ones:

- **Provides External Control:** No one enjoys feeling out of control, yet the impulsive and hyperactive symptoms of ADHD can create this very sensation. Having a structured environment allows children to gain more external control. This will allow your child to understand what and when an event is happening, creating improved behavior and less anxiety. For instance, if your child's routine involves soccer at 3 p.m. and homework at 5 p.m., they'll learn that soccer time is for releasing high energy, while study time is for focusing and concentrating on tasks.
- **Leads to Fewer Conflicts:** I'm not sure about you, but my family has had way too many arguments, from tripping over discarded shoes on the stairs to last-minute school bake sales and forgotten homework assignments. Implementing strict routines can take the stress and anxiety out of your day. Picture an organized house with a schedule for every member, making less time for chaos and more space for enjoyment.

- **Builds Skills and Habits:** Building a strong set of life skills for children with ADHD is super important, as they often miss out on this essential step in childhood. Getting your little one familiar with cleaning routines, self-care, and exercise will promote a healthy lifestyle.
- **Applies to the Whole Family:** A structured household means everyone has a routine. From waking up on time to completing a set list of responsibilities, holding everyone accountable for their own schedules will make for a much more tranquil and loving home. It also means that your little one won't feel so left out!
- **Builds a Foundation for Success:** When children believe they're messy, unintelligent, or lazy, their self-esteem, confidence, and likelihood of succeeding plummet. Setting routines builds a foundation for success, where your child takes control of their environment and creates a future they deserve. Studying at set hours will show them that they are capable; practicing self-care will boost their self-esteem, and maintaining a clean bedroom will build a lifetime of healthy habits.

Your child knows what to expect in a structured environment, allowing them to learn positive behavioral and emotional responses. Creating routines and implementing schedules offers your child the tools to succeed!

ESTABLISHING AN EFFECTIVE ROUTINE AT HOME

Now that we know children with ADHD thrive with routines, all that's left is to establish a detailed yet realistic schedule. While we could pick apart every moment of our child's day, let's start by identifying the three most important areas: the morning, after school, and bedtime. Beginning with small steps will help implement new routines with ease and tranquility. Let's get to it!

Morning Routine

A morning routine is the best place to start, as this dictates the tone of your child's day. As a parent, your number one priority for the morning rush should be to reduce stress and anxiety. I know this is probably easier said than done, as you may also have a job to get to or other little ones to care for. However, a well-crafted routine, where clothes are laid out the night before, a nutritious breakfast is prepped, and school bags are packed, will help tremendously. Rather than your child stumbling down the stairs with their hair in a ball and their bag half-packed, picture a morning when they calmly wake up, practice self-care, and even engage in mindfulness. Trust me, it's completely possible!

A healthy morning routine may look similar to the following:

- **6:30 a.m.—Parents wake up.**
- **6:40 a.m.— Parents prepare breakfast.** If your child isn't a fan of overnight oats or homemade muffins, you'll need some time to prepare breakfast in the morning. While preparing breakfast, lay out a self-care checklist in the bathroom and ensure your child's outfit is ready.
- **7:00 a.m.—Wake up your child.** Gently wake up your child and remind them of the time using a timer or alarm. Be mindful that they may need a couple of reminders to help them get out of bed!
- **7:05 a.m.—Breakfast.** Serve your child's breakfast at the table. Ensure a nutritious meal that helps with concentration and energy. We'll examine this further in the following chapter.

- **7:15 a.m.—Wash up in the bathroom.** Now it's time for your child to use the toilet, brush their teeth, wash their face, and follow a self-care routine. Depending on your child's age, you may need to double-check that they've completed this step; many of our little ones avoid their toothbrush like the plague!
- **7:20 a.m.—Get dressed and practice positive affirmations or mindfulness.**
- **7:35 a.m.—Gather belongings, do a final check, then the departure.** Help your child gather their belongings, which should be kept in the same spot near the door. Use a list with words or pictures of the items they need to leave the house (shoes, jacket, backpack, lunch box, etc.) and leave for school.

Remember that you must adjust this schedule to your child's school time and personal needs. You should also avoid stimulating devices such as the TV, mobile phones, or gaming consoles.

After-School Routine

So, your child has just gotten home from school; they're hungry, not paying attention to a word you say, and will probably bounce off the walls after eating an assortment of snacks. Oh, the joys of parenting! Every child has their own set of needs after school; some may want attention and desperately need to run off some energy in the garden or at an afterschool club, while others may be ready to jump into study time. Either way, a healthy after-school routine can look something like this:

- **3:30 p.m.—Pick up from school.**
- **3:45 p.m.—Enter the home and unpack belongings.**
  Have a clear, set place where your child places their shoes,

backpack, and jacket. Use hooks, labels, and checklists to help them remember. This is also a great time to clean out their lunchbox and prepare it for the following day.
- **3:50 p.m.—Eat a snack.** Offer a nutritious snack to help them recharge after school.
- **4:00 p.m.—Play outdoor or do 15 minutes of indoor movement.** This will help your child burn off some energy and increase focus during study time.
- **4:15 p.m.—Complete homework.** Have a predetermined, tidy space for homework. Set a visual timer for how long they are expected to work to help them focus and manage time effectively. Even if your child wasn't given homework, 30 minutes of reading, quizzes, or online study can help boost their education and create a consistent routine.
- **5:00 p.m.—Have free time/preferred play activity.** Reward them with their favorite activity once they've finished their homework. This helps them have something to work toward when completing homework and provides a positive end to the structured part of their routine.

You may follow this up with a consistent dinnertime routine involving setting the table, eating together as a family, and washing dishes.

Bedtime Routine

This is one of the most important routines, as you'll want to ensure your child gets at least eight hours of sleep. Consider implementing a routine similar to the one below:

- **7:00 p.m.—It's bath time.** Start the evening with a warm bath to help your child relax and wind down from the day.

- **7:30 p.m.—Change into pajamas.** Spend time playing a quiet, relaxing game or reading a book together to continue winding down.
- **7:35 p.m.—Play a relaxing game or read a book.** Help your child change into their pajamas, creating a sense of routine and signaling that bedtime is approaching.
- **8:00 p.m.—Brush teeth.** Ensure your child brushes their teeth thoroughly.
- **8:10 p.m.—Read books.** Read a book to help your child relax and prepare for sleep.
- **8:20 p.m.—Set a time for lights out.** Set a timer for how many minutes until bedtime, making it clear and consistent when it's time for lights out.
- **8:30 p.m.—Put lights out.** Say goodnight and turn off the lights, ensuring a calm and quiet environment for your child to fall asleep.

Remember, you must ensure enough time for your child to relax and unwind. This may mean spending more time talking, reading, and engaging in self-care.

Tips and Tricks for Setting an Effective Routine

Picking up healthy habits and adopting new routines is bound to be tricky; however, this doesn't mean it's impossible. To make this new transition easier on both you and your child, consider the following factors:

- **Understand your child's needs.** A child with ADHD has unique needs that others don't. This could include heightened morning anxiety before school, pent-up energy causing disturbed sleep, or difficulty focusing while completing homework. Whatever the issue is, apply a solution-oriented mindset and determine how a routine can improve it. Perhaps your child needs an extra 15 minutes of talking time and emotional support during the mornings to reduce overwhelm. Maybe they need to apply the Pomodoro technique for homework hours or less stimulation after school. Understand your child's weaknesses and preferences to help build a practical routine.

- **Set realistic goals.** Remember, we're not striking for gold; we're simply trying to reduce stress and improve consistency. This means that your routines should be realistic and easy to follow. Your child will not magically pick up habits like organization or focus; these will take time, practice, and hard work before they can be seamlessly integrated. Ensuring each goal is small and specific will help your child achieve it.
- **Balance activities and downtime.** Just as you need a warm, relaxing bath at night to destress, your child needs fun, engaging activities and downtime. A healthy routine involves a balance between discipline and spontaneity. Encourage them to join clubs, play instruments, draw, and practice sports. Don't forget that your child can have just as much fun while winding down for bed. Calming music, meditation, books, and cuddles with pets are ideal!
- **Build in flexibility.** Life has a funny way of turning out, meaning that some days, your routines simply won't go according to plan. Even 20 minutes of traffic could throw your entire after-school schedule out of whack. As a parent, you have to be prepared for these situations and learn to modify routines as needed. These are also excellent opportunities to teach your child the importance of resilience and adaptability.

The Importance of Visual Aids

If you have a child with ADHD, chances are you've heard other parents, coaches, and even medical professionals emphasize the importance of visual aids. But when it comes to actually implementing them, it can sometimes feel like they're not having any effect on your child. Instead of helping, your child might end up even more confused, staring at your stick figure drawing, unsure whether it's eating cereal or brushing their hair.

Honestly, you're not alone; some ADHD strategies, like visual aids, take a bit of practice and creativity to truly work. But, as a result, your child gains the clarity they need to succeed. Children with ADHD have poor working memories, meaning that retaining simple information can be tricky, especially when it comes to tedious, mundane tasks such as chores or homework. Offering visual aids and clear instructions supports their memory and offers them the tools they need to carry out the task. It can also serve as the following:

- A prompt to begin or persist with a task.
- A cue to refocus on a task after being distracted.
- A model for how to manage emotions.
- A source of motivation to complete a task.
- An external memory aid to remind them of the next step.

This only scratches the surface; your child will also benefit from a surplus of long-term advantages. But if you really want visuals to work, you can't just show them a picture and expect them to understand. The trick is to stick to the three golden principles of visual aids:

1. **Create visuals that are specific.** The key is to be highly specific and consider any learning or cognitive difficulties your child has. For a child with ADHD, this may mean that a cartoon while completing their homework is too overstimulating or a list of written instructions is easily forgettable.
2. **Collaborate with your child.** If your child is at an appropriate age to discuss their learning, then collaborating with them is an awesome idea. Your child will probably be able to identify a couple of things that work well and don't work well for them; they may even want to help you create your own and find the perfect match!
3. **Phase out visuals when they are not needed anymore.** While visuals are great, your child doesn't need them for every task. Consider using them only for the activities they tend to struggle with, like homework or brushing their teeth. This way, they won't become dependent on them or expect them to be shown at school. Eventually, you'll also be able to slowly phase out the usage of visuals, such as when your child gets familiar with a morning routine and knows what to do off the top of their head.

These three golden principles will help your child get the most out of visuals and boost their learning. Now, all that is left is to master the art of teaching visuals; don't worry, it's not as challenging as it sounds. The "SHORRR Fire Way" method is one of the easiest and most practical ways to demonstrate visuals. Try picking up a visual and practicing the following strategy:

- **Show Me:** The first step to teaching a visual is showing your child the cue and explaining it with positive language. You could say something along the lines of "I've noticed you've been struggling with your morning routine; how about we use visuals to make it easier?" Then, you can follow through by picking up each self-care visual and explaining what the child can see, such as "What looks like the first step? Is the boy in the picture brushing his teeth? That's right; you have to pick up your toothbrush, put toothpaste on it, and brush all your teeth until they are clean. Now, what should we do?." This avoids any confusion.

- **Help Me:** Now it's time to help your child with the activity to ensure they genuinely know what they are doing. Hand it over to them and support them where necessary. If they go to brush their teeth but forget to add toothpaste, gently remind them to look back at the visual for guidance.
- **Observe Me:** As your child uses visuals in their daily routine, you'll want to pay close attention but from a distance. If your child is in the bathroom cleaning their teeth, perhaps you can fold laundry in a nearby bedroom or tidy the hallway. Make it known that you're present and there to help if needed without giving direct support.
- **Remind Me:** Visual aids are great at aiding in memory recall, but there are moments when not even the toothbrush will help your child remember what they're supposed to do. Plus, if your child doesn't enjoy the activity at hand, chances are they will avoid it at all costs. You may need to step in now and then to give your child a little push and remind them that they need to follow their routine or that the visuals are there to guide them.
- **Review:** Children with ADHD have interest-based minds, meaning that unless they care about the activity at hand, they're going to act as if it doesn't exist. This may mean that a visual aid may work great for one week but doesn't do so well for the following week.

Reviewing them frequently, switching up pictures, and moving their location will help keep your child engaged. You may need to add a more detailed picture or challenge them with less detail. You can even ask your child what would make the chore more interesting.
- **Reward:** Most importantly, you'll need to reward your child for all their hard work. An ADHD mind struggles to feel motivation unless it's rewarded almost instantly. Keep verbally encouraging them and offering tokens toward your family's new token economy!

By following these steps, you are bound to create successful and effective routines. All that is left is a bit of patience and consistency to see incredible results.

ADHD-FRIENDLY ENVIRONMENT

Unless your child has a passion for feng shui, chances are they're messy and unorganized, which is to be expected. Children with ADHD tend to be a bit messier than the average neurotypical child. This is because their brain's weak executive function makes cleaning up and staying organized challenging; even managing their school books and sweaters can be difficult. Plus, their brains aren't exactly excited to clean the dishes or tidy their bedroom, so they won't care to remember it.

While children with ADHD struggle to organize, this doesn't mean they're exempt from the dreaded dishwasher duty or a nice Sunday bedroom sweep. Good hygiene and basic cleanliness are essential to a healthy and productive future. So, how can we get our little ones to put effort into their environment? Let's take a look:

- **Use labels**. A label maker can genuinely change the game. Think of labels as simple instructions, telling your child what goes where. If your child has three baskets labeled for clothes, toys, and school materials, cleaning their bedroom becomes ten times easier. Remember to keep labels simple and easy to read.
- **Simplify containers.** I'm not sure about you, but my child's closet was a disaster until I started implementing simplified containers. Socks, underwear, vests, hats, and even gloves had chaotically claimed an entire drawer. Hence, dividing them each into their own little container made my life far less stressful. Consider simplifying big storage containers to eliminate clutter.
- **Minimize location used.** Every item in your house should have a home. Toys, stuffed animals, hair accessories, and school books should be kept in your child's bedroom. Explain to them that their bedroom is their own mini apartment, where they're responsible for keeping their belongings clean and organized. This will also offer them independence, something many kids crave. Remember that certain items, such as dirty shoes or a game console, should not belong in the bedroom.
- **Use clear bins.** When it comes to organizing storage, you'll want to choose the right bins. Typically, I opt for clear bins, as they allow children to see what is inside the container without rummaging through it. This avoids stress and confusion at cleanup times.
- **Use color codes.** If you've ever spoken to a child, you'll know they love rainbows, making these storage options fun and inclusive. Color-coding your storage bins or containers for clothes, books, and toys will make it more enticing for your child to organize their bedrooms, saving you from tantrums and meltdowns over cleaning!

I can't promise that these five tips and tricks will make your child magically want to clean, but they will definitely make it far less stressful and an easier job to complete.

TIME BLINDNESS AND TIME MANAGEMENT

ADHD and time have a bit of an unstable relationship. Let me explain: Typically, the human body reacts to external information like our environment's light, sound, and smell to gauge what time it is. While we may not be able to pinpoint the hour, it gives us a good sense of direction as to the time of the day, how much time has passed, and what we're to expect later in the day. For children with ADHD, this perception is disrupted, resulting in time blindness.

Time blindness is a hallmark symptom of ADHD, characterized by an inability to gauge how much time has passed and estimate how much time is needed to do certain things. If your child is under the age of ten, you may not have had an opportunity to witness this symptom yet, as you'd typically manage their day for them. But this doesn't mean that time blindness isn't a legitimate issue that requires attention. Time blindness can seriously impair your child's day, as they commonly struggle with the following factors:

- **Time Perception or Estimation:** This is the skill of estimating how much time has passed. It also means knowing how long it will take to finish a task.
- **Time Horizon:** This helps us understand how soon a task needs to be started. People with ADHD often have a short time horizon and "future time blindness," so they might not notice deadlines until it's too late.

- **Time Management:** Time management involves planning and organizing how much time to spend on different tasks and activities. It's a complex skill involving focus, memory, and planning, all of which are difficult for people with ADHD.
- **Time Sequencing:** This is the ability to put events or tasks in the order they happened.
- **Time Reproduction:** This means being able to do something again for the same amount of time as before.

Practicing games based on time, as well as placing clocks, alarms, and timers around the house, will set the perfect foundation for improving time blindness. There are also a few strategies you can try out to help your little one along the way:

- **Move beyond "now/not now" thinking.** This strategy involves helping your child consider both the past and the future. Ask your child to talk about what they did at school or their plans with grandparents on the weekend. For older kids, try talking about an upcoming party or a movie trip. You can also involve them in planning activities like a BBQ or a craft project.
- **Teach time estimation skills.** Practice estimating how long activities take by timing things you do together, like walking to school or baking cookies. You can even involve a little reward for the person closest to the minute. This helps your child understand how long tasks really take and plan accordingly.
- **Show how to budget time.** Sit with your child to plan out tasks like homework or piano practice. Discuss their time estimates and provide feedback. Add extra time for unexpected delays, and set alarms to remind them of deadlines.

Keep in mind that developing time management habits takes time and practice. Always celebrate your little ones' small successes and encourage them to keep up the good work!

CREATE A VISUAL SCHEDULE

Along with the "SHORRR Fire Way" method, you'll need to include written instructions. Whether your child can or can't follow timetables, visualizing one will allow them to get familiar with the practice and hold the entire family accountable. Below, you will find a simple schedule and reward system:

Time	Activity	Notes	Tokens Collected

Remember that this does not replace visual aids; consistently following the SHORR method will offer the best results and help younger ones build healthy habits. You can adapt the template to your needs and even get creative by using a whiteboard or colorful poster. Keep it clear and easy to read with an abundance of pictures. Before you know it, your child will have routines and schedules down to a tee!

JOURNALING FOR SELF-REFLECTION

Wow! Routines, schedules, and organization truly do pay off. Before we wrap up this chapter, hit the pause button and grab your journals and pens for a tranquil moment of introspection. Remember, consistency is key to success in all areas of life, even journaling. So, let's further our progress and answer the following questions openly and honestly:

1. How do you recharge your mind and body? How can you improve upon this and create a regular self-care routine?
2. What piece of advice would you give another parent?
3. What makes your child feel most loved? How can you include this in your family's new schedule?
4. Name one thing that is holding you back and preventing you from being the best parent to your child. What actionable steps can you take to improve it?
5. List three qualities about yourself that make you a proud parent.

CULTIVATE PHYSICAL WELL-BEING

> *That's the other thing: Even if you're on medication, you still have to treat your body properly and take care of yourself. The idea that ADHD goes away or you grow out of it isn't true.*
>
> — TY PENNINGTON

You may not want to hear this, but your child's lifestyle may not be doing them any good. Picture a healthy and happy lifestyle as having three pillars: nutrition, sleep, and exercise. Without these pillars, you welcome poor mental health, a low quality of life, and severe symptoms of ADHD. Without further ado, let's ditch unhealthy habits and adopt life-changing practices!

NUTRITION

Whether you're an adult or a child, the brain requires nutrients for energy production and cell repair. Without a healthy and balanced diet, we simply wouldn't be able to function adequately. For children with ADHD, nutrition is ten times more important, as they easily adopt poor dietary habits and may even be experiencing severe symptoms due to aggravating ingredients. While changing your child's diet isn't easy, maintaining a balanced diet is key to a happy and healthy lifestyle. Despite swapping chocolate for fruit and chicken nuggets for leafy greens being a headache, it is totally worth it!

Foods to Include in an ADHD Diet

While there is no specific diet for ADHD, highly nutritious foods can help manage your child's ADHD symptoms as well as support their emotional and physical growth. Below, you'll find a list of recommended foods for children with ADHD:

- **Protein:** Protein is essential for children as it increases the production of neurotransmitters, which are important chemical messengers in the brain used to enhance focus, attention, and even tranquility. You'll want to avoid whey protein derived from cows, as it often contains herbicides and pesticides. Opt for grass-fed, pasture-raised, organic eggs, fish, poultry, and lean beef. Nuts and beans are also a great source of protein.
- **Complex Carbohydrates:** Carbs aren't all bad. Complex carbohydrates such as sweet potatoes, beets, brown rice, and quinoa can positively impact the ADHD brain by producing serotonin. This will help regulate your child's mood, leading to emotional stability. Unlike traditional carbs, complex carbohydrates are rich in fiber and digest slowly, which will avoid rapid emotional changes.
- **Omega-3 Fatty Acids:** Children with ADHD often have low levels of omega-3 fatty acids in their brains, meaning they miss out on vital nutrients for brain growth. To

reduce ADHD symptoms, try including sardines, salmon, sea bass, crustaceans, and plant-based foods such as chia seeds, flax seeds, walnuts, and soybeans in your child's diet.
- **Iron:** A common belief among researchers is that iron can contribute to ADHD symptoms. This means that iron supplements may contribute to more productive and healthier behavior. However, your child must get their iron levels checked before you administer any iron supplements, as high dosages can be dangerous.
- **Zinc:** Zinc can help regulate the release of dopamine, the feel-good hormone often lacking in ADHD brains. According to Frye (2017), research has concluded that regularly consuming zinc supplements or foods such as beef, spinach, and pumpkin seeds can help reduce the intensity of hyperactivity and impulsivity.
- **Magnesium:** Magnesium offers a calming effect on the mind and contributes to healthy neurotransmitter functioning. Consider adding dark leafy greens, nuts, seeds, and beans to your child's diet.
- **B-vitamins:** When children become deficient in B6 vitamins, it can cause severe irritability and fatigue. On the other hand, sufficient B6 vitamins can reduce anxiety and stress while increasing alertness. I'm not sure about you, but I'll definitely be adding wild-caught tuna, bananas, spinach, and salmon to my little ones' diet.

In all honesty, switching up your child's diet can be quite a challenge. Most children and teens prefer a plate of beige chicken nuggets and fries rather than a nutritious variety of veggies and high-quality protein. For this reason, it's important that you don't overwhelm yourself; try to focus less on restricting foods and more on choosing healthy options that increase your child's joy. Organic seasonings and homemade sauces can spice up bland dishes and make them appear more appetizing to your little one. You can even involve your child and ask them to help you look for healthy alternatives while grocery shopping. Who knows, they may even reach for a bag of fresh fruit!

Foods to Avoid in an ADHD Diet

Just as we've added nutritious ingredients into our diets, we'll also need to remove a few unhealthy ones. The following foods are notorious contributors to ADHD, aggravating symptoms and leading to an unhealthy lifestyle. Let's take a look:

- **Refined or Simple Carbohydrates:** Unlike complex carbohydrates, refined carbohydrates are highly processed and removed from their natural form. This means that they have little to no nutritional value. Try to avoid packaged chips, crackers, and fruit snacks.
- **Caffeine:** While you may think that a glass of soda or a soothing tea may enhance your child's focus, it can have the opposite effect. One study by Blanchfield (2023) discovered that regularly consuming high quantities of caffeine with ADHD can lead to the development of more ADHD symptoms and a lower quality of life. Not only is caffeine damaging to your child's mental well-being, but it is also toxic.
- **Food Additives:** While additives have never been healthy, certain food dyes, such as red and yellow, have been linked to the onset of ADHD (Children's Environmental Health Center 2020). Blue food dye is also thought to intensify ADHD symptoms. Always refer to the ingredient label when buying food and opt for items with minimal ingredients and chemical-sounding words like red dye #40.

- **Sugar:** We all love a sweet treat, but not when it comes to the cost of obesity and deadly diseases such as cancer and diabetes. Sugar can cause surges of energy followed by crashes; this may disrupt bedtime routines, productivity, and emotional regulation.

SLEEP

Did you know that up to 70 percent of children with ADHD suffer from sleep-related disorders? While you may not want to hear this, your child is at high risk of developing sleep deprivation. It's one of those pesky ADHD manifestations that no one ever tells you about. But don't worry, together we're going to get to the bottom of it!

Every household experiences bedtime tantrums; it's a rarity for your child to be eager to get to bed on time. However, a consistent pattern of trouble staying asleep, frequently waking up during the night, and resisting bedtime may need to be examined further. It's also important to bear in mind that every child is unique, meaning that they may demonstrate symptoms differently from others. Here are a few of the most common signs of sleep-related disorders in children with ADHD:

- **Bedtime Resistance:** Does your child frequently beg you for an extra hour before bedtime? Do they cry and plead with you to stay awake for longer? Or experience difficulty settling into bed for the night? If they do, this may be a sign of poor sleep.
- **Bedtime Anxiety:** It's normal for a child with ADHD to experience stress and anxiety as a result of their symptoms. However, if nighttime worries, such as a fear of

the dark or an overactive mind, are getting the best of them, this could be an indicator of anxiety.
- **Insomnia:** That's right, insomnia can affect children just as it does adults. If you notice your child struggling to fall asleep or stay asleep, this may be a sign of insomnia. You may have noticed them wandering around upstairs as if it weren't bedtime or even waking you up in the early hours of the morning.
- **Delayed Sleep:** If you've passed the evening tantrums and now have a tween or teen, then they may experience delayed sleep. This involves feeling tired in the early hours of the morning but wide awake at night.

Any child, whether they have ADHD or not, requires at least eight hours of sleep per night; if not, they may experience detrimental side effects to their physical and emotional well-being. Take a look below at the following possible consequences of sleep deprivation:

- Intensified symptoms of ADHD
- Increased risk of depression, anxiety, and obesity
- A lower quality of life
- Difficulty functioning during the day
- Irritability and restlessness
- A low school attendance rate

There isn't an exact reason why children with ADHD experience such difficulty sleeping; some doctors believe it's down to stimulant medication, while others say it's a concoction of high stress, anxiety, and depression. Despite the cause being unknown, this doesn't mean it can't be helped. In fact, there are various ways you can improve your child's sleep cycle:

- **Shut down screens.** Electronics are extremely stimulating. TVs, phones, iPads, computers, and gaming consoles should be shut off at least 30 minutes before bedtime. Make sure to direct your child toward a more relaxing activity, such as reading a book or taking a warm bath.
- **Keep a routine.** Remember, consistency is key for children with ADHD. Consider referring back to the previous chapter for practical and effective advice on setting nighttime routines.
- **Limit caffeine.** Sodas, teas, coffees, and any other beverage high in sugar or caffeine should be cut out from your child's diet. These drinks tend to charge their batteries and keep them awake for longer than needed.
- **Try white noise.** Don't knock it till you try it. White noise can be super relaxing and offers a calming environment for your child.
- **Make sure they move.** If you want your child to get a good night's sleep, then exercise is paramount for releasing energy.

Nothing is impossible, not even fixing a child, tween, or teen's sleep schedule. Slowly but steadily, you'll find your child less resistant, anxious, and stressed at bedtime. Good luck!

PHYSICAL ACTIVITY

While you may be tired and ready to hit the hay as soon as the sun goes down, your little one may still need to burn off a bit of energy. Children with ADHD are notorious bundles of joy with heaps of energy, so why not put that youthful spirit to good use? Exercise offers tons of benefits:

- **Burns Up Excess Energy:** Does your child ever go to bed with too much energy? Do they often appear restless and hyped? Well, that may be because they haven't burnt off enough energy throughout the day. Whether it's running in the garden or playing soccer with friends, exercise can help your child get a better night's sleep.
- **Improves Mood:** Exercise can support positive behavior by reducing anxiety, aggression, and social problems, leading to a happier and healthier child.
- **Promotes Dopamine Release:** Children with ADHD tend to have low levels of dopamine in their brains, making exercise a fundamental part of their day. Exercise is a reliable way to promote dopamine release and improve emotional regulation. It can even have the same effect as some stimulant medications!
- **Can Improve Executive Function:** It's no secret that children with ADHD have difficulty focusing, organizing, remembering, and multitasking because of poor executive functioning. However, exercise may just be the key to improving these symptoms. A study conducted by Herndon (2018) successfully concluded that sixty-one adults with ADHD were able to improve their executive functioning through exercise.

Once you start, you really won't be able to stop; weekend hikes, after-school bike riding, and morning jogs are fun and healthy activities for the entire family. You can also try getting your child involved with local sports clubs or getting a gym membership for your teen!

FIVE-DAY MEAL PLAN

So, you want to begin making deliciously nutritious meals for your entire family but aren't sure where to start? No problem; I've got your back. Below, you will find a seven-day meal plan that supports healthy young minds as well as ADHD. Feel free to make adjustments where necessary, especially if your little one has any food intolerances or allergies. Enjoy!

	Breakfast	**Lunch**	**Dinner**	**Snacks**
Monday	Scrambled eggs with a sprinkle of cheese and spinach A bowl of fruit	Tuna melt on whole wheat bread with vegetables A side of fruit	Baked chicken with seasoned vegetables and potatoes with the skins	Oatmeal and fresh fruit
Tuesday	Overnight oats with fresh fruit	Leafy green salad topped with fresh, diced tomatoes, shredded cheese, and grilled chicken or salmon cut into strips	Homemade beef chili	Hard-boiled eggs with tomatoes
Wednesday	Fresh fruit smoothie with Greek yogurt, protein powder, chia seeds, and ice	Cheeseburger with a whole wheat bun and a side of vegetables or fruit	Whole wheat pasta with chicken and spinach	Nuts with cubed cheese and deli ham
Thursday	Ham, egg, and cheese sandwich with whole wheat bread	Chicken, lettuce, tomato, and cheese whole wheat wrap	Grilled pork chops with brown rice and roasted vegetables	Hummus and carrots or celery
Friday	Oatmeal with fresh or frozen berries and chia seeds	Chicken burrito protein bowl	Baked fish with grilled vegetables	Nuts and fresh fruit

Saturday	Cheese, spinach, and tomato omelet	Chicken, lettuce, tomato, and cheese whole wheat wrap	Stir-fried chicken with brown rice	Cheese on whole wheat crackers and apple slices
Sunday	Greek yogurt with berries and nuts	Seasoned grilled chicken breast with a side salad or fruit	Whole wheat pasta with fresh spaghetti sauce and meatballs	Trail mix and dark chocolate

JOURNALING FOR SELF-REFLECTION

Now that you know how to create a healthier and happier lifestyle for your entire family, it's time to implement these tips and tricks. Consider using the journaling prompts below to help build consistency and iron out any kinks:

1. What are your current daily routines and habits as a family?
2. Which three habits do you feel are beneficial, and which three habits could use improvement?
3. How can you make small changes to enhance your family's overall well-being?
4. What obstacles does your family face in maintaining healthy habits?
5. What resources or support systems can you rely on to help your family stay on track?

No Parent Is an Island

"One of the marvelous things about community is that it enables us to welcome and help people in a way we couldn't as individuals."

— JEAN VANIER

Being a parent is one of the most rewarding journeys, yet it's also one of the most challenging. Add ADHD into the mix, and it's easy to start second-guessing every decision you make and feeling guilty when you think it might have been the wrong one. This can be very isolating, and sometimes it feels like no other parent understands what you're going through. But the global prevalence of childhood ADHD is thought to be around 5% (National Institute for Health and Care Excellence, 2024) – and that shows there are many other parents in the same boat.

My goal in writing this book was to bring you the tools you need to make this journey a little easier, and I want to reach as many people as I can. Not just to give them these strategies, but to remind them that they're not alone and that other parents are facing the same struggles. That alone is a very powerful thing – it's more difficult to doubt yourself when you realize other people are plagued with the same worries.

It's with this in mind that I'd like to ask for your help in getting this book out to more of the parents who need it. How? It's surprisingly easy. All it takes is a short review.

By leaving a review of this book on Amazon, you'll show other parents where they can find the guidance they're looking for – and you'll remind them that they're part of a large community of parents facing the same challenges.

People are searching for this information, and your review will help them find it quickly and easily – which, as I'm sure you know, is necessary when you're a busy parent.

Thank you so much for your support. There's no doubting the power of community, and with your help, I can support far more families.

EMOTIONAL RESILIENCE BEYOND MEASURE

> *ADHD is real and valid. The sooner we recognize the patterns and learn to work with these kids, the better assured we will be that they, as adults, will be healthy members of society.*
>
> — RHONDA VAN DIEST

One of the scariest things you have to do as a parent is allow your child to be independent; one day, they're asking for cuddles, and the next, they're moving out. And the worst part is that the time goes by in a blink of an eye. While we can't rewind the clock or force our children to stay little forever, we can set them up for a successful future. We can give them the tools they need to find fulfilling jobs, maintain healthy relationships, and convert their dreams into reality. You'll find it's easier than you think!

EMOTIONAL DYSREGULATION AND ADHD

At a glance, emotional dysregulation can appear minor, with a few tantrums here and there and maybe one or two more crying sessions than expected. However, emotional dysregulation goes far beyond what meets the eye. It involves an impaired ability to control your emotional response, creating extreme emotions for something that doesn't fit the situation. For example, your child's favorite TV show may end, and they may begin to cry uncontrollably, struggling to calm down. As you can see, the child's behavior went from 0 to 100. Following are some of the key symptoms of emotional dysregulation:

- Emotional responses that appear disproportionate to their triggers
- Difficulty soothing oneself, even when recognizing the overreaction
- Limited patience for frustration or irritation
- Issues with anger or unexpected outbursts
- Tendency to experience emotions as overwhelmingly intense
- Trouble shifting focus away from the emotional state

If you don't have ADHD, it can feel as if your child is almost overreacting or being dramatic, which is why it's so important to recognize that their brains function differently from neurotypical ones. It's challenging for their minds to look past what has happened and redirect their focus until the situation has been entirely resolved. Unfortunately, this can impact your child's future more than you may realize. For instance:

- **Difficulty in Relationships and Friendships:** Emotional dysregulation can feel unpredictable and overwhelming to others. Whether it's friendships or romantic relationships, managing your emotions is the key to success; impulsivity and outbursts tend to frighten people away.
- **Difficulty in Academic Settings:** Schools, colleges, and universities often require lots of organization and focus, which doesn't come easy to those with ADHD. Due to the difficulty of meeting these high demands, your child may struggle with stress, intensifying their emotional dysregulation. Not to mention that exam season comes with pressure, meaning self-care is often put on the back burner.
- **Difficulty with Daily Activities:** Self-care rituals, daily routines, and work tasks can be tedious and demanding. When an emotional response is triggered, all of these rituals and routines are practically tossed in the trash until the issue is resolved. Hence, maintaining employment and taking care of oneself is often unsuccessful.
- **Difficulty with Self-Esteem:** Most of the time, children, teens, and adults with ADHD are aware that their emotions are out of proportion to the situation. Feeling stuck and unable to manage their feelings can lead to shame, guilt, and self-blame. This can take a serious toll on your child's mental and physical health.

While the cause of emotional dysregulation in individuals with ADHD isn't entirely understood, a recent study has revealed new findings. According to Hebert (2023), brain scans have demonstrated that an overactive amygdala and an underactive prefrontal cortex may lead to emotional dysregulation. The amygdala is responsible for emotions and can react strongly even to small triggers, while the prefrontal cortex, which regulates emotions, may not work well due to low dopamine levels. This imbalance is thought to contribute to emotional regulation problems in ADHD.

EMOTIONAL REGULATION STRATEGIES

While a chemical imbalance in the brain may cause emotional dysregulation, that doesn't mean it can't be helped; after all, everything has a solution. Breaking the cycle of unpredictable negative emotions will involve developing emotional regularity. This is the ability to control your own emotional state by rethinking the situation at hand to limit feelings of anger, sadness, or anxiety. It's not the easiest thing to do, but with practice and time comes awesome focus and positivity.

When our children are young, outbursts and tantrums are to be expected. However, as they grow older, this behavior becomes less and less acceptable. Adults are expected to be able to manage their behavior, and if not, it can lead to unemployment, few to no friends, or mental health concerns. We've all regretted saying something we wish had never left our mouths; now, picture your child as an adult, experiencing that very same feeling of shame and guilt nearly every week. I bet you're worried, aren't you?

As a parent, you have the power to shape your child's future and direct their actions and behavior in a positive light. Even if your child is reaching puberty or already in high school, their minds are like sponges, ready to soak up any positive input you have. With this being said, let's empower our children to do better with the following emotional regulation skills:

- **Consider their developmental level.** Children with ADHD tend to be two to three years mentally below their actual age. For example, a ten-year-old with ADHD may behave more like a seven-year-old due to their developmental level. When considering how to react or talk to your child during outbursts and tantrums, you must take into account their developmental level rather than their age.

- **Provide as much consistency and stability as possible.** Just as children with ADHD need consistency with routines, they also require predictable behavior from you as the parent. Using consistent limits, rules, boundaries, and rewards will help your child gain stability.
- **Provide support where they tend to struggle the most.** Identifying behavioral patterns will help you tremendously with inserting consistent rules and rewards. Try to identify when, where, and why your child typically has outbursts. Then, you can put the necessary tools in place to help them succeed.
- **Help them understand their feelings.** We all experience big emotions, but that doesn't mean we're all equipped to deal with them. Teaching your child to identify emotions and triggers can increase self-awareness. Over time, they'll learn to react with words rather than raw and impulsive emotions. Consider talking about your own emotions and telling your child how you deal with them, encouraging them to identify their own feelings, and modeling good self-control.
- **Set up quiet spaces.** On top of emotional validation, creating a relaxing and calming environment will offer a safe space for your child to express intense emotions and calm down. You can even label it as their own little retreat, stocked up with cozy pillows and blankets, books, fidget toys, and teddies.
- **Build their emotional awareness with feeling charts.** When your child is overwhelmed, upset, and practically choking on their tears, it can be hard for them to put their

words into practice. A feelings chart is a visual aid with cartoon emotions ranging from one to five. In heated moments, you can pull out the feelings chart and allow your child to identify how they're feeling; this will self-validate their emotions, leading to less dependency on you.
- **Use countdowns for self-regulation.** As we know, their emotions can go from 0 to 100 in seconds, making self-regulation an incredibly important tool. Teaching them strategies that they can use when they're alone or at school will allow them more independence and reduce their anxiety. The countdown method involves slowly counting from ten down to zero while imagining a happy place such as the park, Disney World, or anything that brings joy to your child; it is a simple yet effective tool.

Providing your child with emotional validation and practical tools will help build a foundation for emotional regulation. Remember to be patient—it will take time for your child to convert negative patterns of behavior and intense emotions into honest and empathetic words. Trust me, consistency pays off!

MINDFULNESS

Mindfulness is a meditative technique used to redirect judgment and negativity while enhancing awareness. Our little ones tend to get so caught up in their busy minds that feelings of anxiety, stress, and overwhelm completely take over. With mindfulness, your child can reflect on their feelings, calming their emotional and physical responses. Over time, poor coping mechanisms such as screaming and crying will be replaced with control and self-awareness.

Unlike traditional forms of meditation, where your child might be expected to sit as still as possible, mindfulness is interactive and fun. Your child can learn to manage their emotions and thoughts while practicing deep breathing or noticing their environment's colors, shapes, and textures. Even better, it offers measurable results; Lee et al. (2022) gathered statistical data from twelve mindfulness studies conducted on children with ADHD and discovered that actively engaging in mindfulness can reduce ADHD symptom intensity. How awesome is that?

Mindfulness Techniques

With an ADHD mind, thoughts and intense emotions can easily lead to overwhelm. That's why it's always best to be prepared with simple yet effective relaxation strategies. Consider implementing the following methods in your home and teaching your child the importance of mindfulness.

7/11 Breathing

1. Begin by taking a deep breath through your mouth. Feel your lungs and stomach expand with air as you hold it for 7 seconds.
2. Now, slowly release the air through your nose for 11 seconds, feeling your stomach contract and decompress.

Mindful Coloring

Children with ADHD are super creative, so why not use it to their advantage? Grab some fun gel pens, colorful pencils, and markers, and encourage your child to notice how they feel while doodling on the paper.

The "I Notice ..." Game

The game "I Notice ..." is similar to "I Spy ..." but with various answers to increase your child's self-awareness. Ask questions based on the colors of the rainbow, textures, or shapes. Chances are they'll remove themselves from their busy minds and notice things they never spotted before in their environment.

FOSTERING EMOTIONAL RESILIENCE

If you've ever been told you have thick skin or know how to roll with the punches, chances are you have great emotional resilience. Simply put, emotional resilience is the ability to easily adapt to stressful situations by using social support and optimism, managing your emotions, and staying resilient. Rather than breaking down and crying from a tough meeting with the boss, you take a deep breath and look at your options going forward.

Children with ADHD naturally have low emotional resilience, as they're often easily overwhelmed and suffer from high levels of anxiety and stress. So, what does this mean for you as a parent? It can suggest that your child is more emotionally dependent on you, constantly seeking out validation and reassurance. They may face more academic setbacks and miss opportunities for growth. Their siblings may even feel neglected because of how much attention is given to the neurodivergent child.

Emotional resilience is key to self-development and a healthy state of mind; without it, your child may grow to suffer from chronic stress and severe anxiety or depression. With this being said, let's take a look at some of the best ways to teach your child emotional resilience:

- **Monitor overall health.** Eating well, getting enough sleep, and exercising are essential for emotional resilience. Developing unhealthy habits, such as a poor sleeping schedule, can make it harder to handle stress and challenges and regulate emotions.
- **Understand and manage triggers.** Social support is crucial for children. Connecting with others and forming supportive and encouraging relationships will help your child build emotional resilience. They'll share experiences, learn compassion, and practice communication, all of which offer opportunities for emotional growth and independence.
- **Identify early warning signs.** Children with ADHD often feel more stress than their neurotypical peers, which can lead to overwhelm and difficulty coping. For example, a child's tantrum may indicate they are overwhelmed and unable to cope. Strengthening coping skills and practicing mindfulness techniques regularly can help manage stress.

Coping Technique: Five-Finger Breathing

There's nothing worse than feeling overwhelmed in a situation you can't get out of. For you, this could be a traffic jam or a three-hour-long meeting; for your child, it may be a school test or a play date. The five-finger breathing technique is the perfect coping strategy for any stressful situation:

1. Begin by placing your hand out in front of you and separating your fingers so there is space between them.
2. Now, hold up the pointer finger from your other hand.
3. Place your pointer finger at the bottom of your thumb and trace up toward the tip, breathing in through your mouth.

4. Now, breathe out through your nose as your pointer finger traces back down your finger.
5. Continue this pattern until you reach your pinky finger.

JOURNALING FOR SELF-REFLECTION

See, I told you setting your child up for success wouldn't be as bad as you thought! Before we move on to our next chapter, where we'll be learning the art of healthy communication, let's take a moment to reflect on all that we have learned. Grab your journals and get ready to answer the following prompts:

1. What makes you feel powerful? How can you help your child feel empowered and confident?
2. How do you encourage yourself to take the first step when you want to try something new? What would you say to your child if they wanted to try a new hobby or activity?
3. How do you embrace authenticity, even if it looks different from what others expect? Do you think your child should embrace their authenticity?
4. How do you forgive yourself when you make mistakes?
5. When do you feel most confident and happiest within your skin? If you don't, how can you improve this and mirror positive behavior to your child?

WORDS THAT CONNECT

> *It is difficult to instruct children because of their natural inattention; the true mode, of course, is to first make our modes interesting to them.*
>
> — JOHN LOCKE

How hard could communicating with a child be? Apparently, it is way more complex than many of us thought. Talking to a child with ADHD often means that they're listening to you but not hearing you—it goes in one ear and straight out of the other. But this isn't their fault; our little ones have poor memory and attention skills. So, it's time for us to level up our parenting game and learn top-tier strategies to help our children become active participants rather than passive listeners!

COMMUNICATION CHALLENGES

Communication challenges? What are those, and what do they have to do with ADHD? Chances are you could list several ways hyperactive, impulsive, and inattentive symptoms affect your child's day-to-day life but struggle to understand ADHD's link to communication struggles. I think it's about time we bridge the gap and take a deeper dive into the core symptoms of ADHD.

If we take a closer look, we can easily see that ADHD has a direct link with communication skills. Some of the core symptoms involve blurting out information, talking excessively, not listening when spoken to, and frequently interrupting, all of which build a poor foundation for healthy communication. Not to mention that these symptoms are often exacerbated by other aspects of ADHD, such as stress and anxiety. You may have even experienced the following situations firsthand:

- Your child doesn't seem to listen when spoken to directly.
- They often blurt out answers.
- They frequently forget to make eye contact.
- They repeatedly overtalk or dominate conversations.
- They're often distracted and not focused, leading to missed social cues.
- Forgetfulness leads to misunderstandings or missed appointments.
- They frequently daydream and space out.
- They speak way too quickly.
- They have difficulty organizing thoughts or getting to the point.
- They tend to misread social cues or misinterpret others' emotions.

- They become easily frustrated or overwhelmed in conversations.

Effective communication often relies on executive function, the mental process that enables us to focus, organize, plan, manage information, and regulate emotions. Think about it: To hold a conversation, we have to pay attention and quickly sort through all the information we're being told while regulating our emotions and behavior. We have to keep calm and manage our replies. We may even need to pick up on social cues and adjust our body language.

Due to a deficit in executive function, children with ADHD lack this essential component. Their brains run a million miles an hour, distracting them from their environment and the conversation. Poor memory skills mean they struggle with retaining information they're being told, making it ten times more difficult to pick up on social cues. They miss the details and can't puzzle together what's happening around them, especially when it comes to those unspoken rules of socializing. Understanding that poor communication skills stem from the symptoms of ADHD is fundamental; it will help reduce stigma, shame, and guilt for both you and your child. Now, all that is left is to implement a practical yet effective solution!

ACTIVE LISTENING

Active listening is more than just hearing words; it's a skill that involves processing information and seeking the meaning and intent behind others' words. In simple terms, it includes all the aspects of healthy communication you desire for your child: being fully present during conversations, showing interest and eye contact, picking up on nonverbal cues, asking questions, and listening to understand rather than just responding. Active listening not only helps your child understand others, but it also demonstrates empathy and compassion. This skill can help them strengthen their relationships and become fully present in the moment. And the best part? It's entirely achievable!

When your child practices active listening, their perception of others and the environment undergoes a profound transformation. It enriches relationships and broadens horizons. The key to unlocking this potential lies in practice: By consistently using techniques to strengthen active listening skills, you can improve your child's executive function. Let's explore the strategies that will help your child develop healthy communication skills:

- **Make the message interactive.** When our little ones are bored or tired, they're less likely to listen to anything we have to say. Spicing up a conversation with fun interactive moments can help grasp your child's attention. For instance, if you want your child to go outside and run off some energy, try getting them up from the sofa and having a little dance with them. If you'd like them to do their homework, pretend to scribble on a piece of paper as if you were solving math questions, or flip through some books to suggest reading time. Have fun with it!
- **Get comfortable with repetition.** Rome wasn't built in a day, nor will your child's listening skills be. Repetition is key for these little bundles of joy, as they'll often forget information and look past the details. Consistently repeating instructions and words without getting frustrated will support and encourage your child to process the information rather than become overwhelmed and stressed.

- **Release pent-up energy.** Children are energetic with or without ADHD; burning some steam and releasing pent-up energy through regular exercise routines will help your child free their mind. It will also help them improve their listening and focus, as those pesky urges to get up and move around will become less apparent.
- **Make them practice eye contact.** Teaching your child the basics of social cues and body language will help them understand the importance of nonverbal communication. Allow them to mirror your actions and copy eye contact and nodding, as this will help them become more familiar with the concept.
- **Encourage them to ask questions.** When we ask questions, it shows others that we're interested in the conversation and value their opinion. This is crucial for building healthy relationships. Consider asking your child to follow up on stories and instructions with questions. Practice at home and allow them to build up the courage and confidence to voice what's on their mind but in a less disruptive manner.
- **Cook with them.** If you want to double up on bonding time and improve your child's communication skills, then cooking or baking is ideal. Read the instructions of a recipe to your child step-by-step, and get them to follow along. This way, they'll practice actively listening and following instructions. You'll even get a tasty dinner or scrumptious sweet treat out of it!
- **Play the "Spot the Change" game.** This is one of my favorite games to play with my child. It's not only fun but also great for strengthening your child's short-term memory. Grab one of your child's favorite books and read a page. Then, read it again while adding new information or changing the storyline. Ask your child to pay close

attention and clap each time they think the story has changed.
- **Play the telephone game.** The telephone game is another awesome activity for your entire family to enjoy. Gather everyone in a circle, and, one at a time, whisper a sentence in each other's ears, changing a word or two as you go. In the end, let your little ones try to figure out how the sentence has changed.

When implementing these strategies, ensure to offer simple yet frequent feedback to your child. It's important to address inappropriate behavior calmly and compassionately. Guide them through understanding social cues and navigating right from wrong. Clearly explaining your expectations and writing them down will help tremendously; visual clues are always best when it comes to implementing routines, instructions, and rules.

PARENT-CHILD HARMONY

As parents, we often underestimate how our words and actions impact our children. The reality is that our little ones, tweens, and even teens are picking up on everything we do, from how we walk to the way we talk. In fact, a study by Runcan et al. (2012) researched the gravity of healthy communication and revealed that the more parents communicate with their children, the more likely the child's social behavior will improve. This means a positive relationship with healthy communication between you and your child could enhance their communication skills and help them relate to others around them. Incredible, isn't it?

The problem is that ADHD and sensory issues can make it tricky for children to grasp what your actions and words really mean, often leaving them confused and creating a false reality. This makes clear communication essential for children with ADHD. Let's take a look at a few ways you can improve your parent-child communication:

- **Give clear, specific directions.** Unfortunately, your child can't read your mind and is likely to feel overwhelmed when an abundance of information is thrown at them. The trick is to be clear and specific when explaining instructions. Always break down tasks and activities into bite-size pieces so your child can focus on one small step at a time. You don't even have to give them all the information at once; you can check back in after 15–20 minutes to update them on the next step.
- **Give your child choices.** It's important to remember that ADHD brains are interest-based; they are hard-wired to remember activities they enjoy and forget that anything else even exists. Offering your child options often gives the illusion that they're interested in the task as if they picked it themselves. This will help them remember instructions or any advice you've given.
- **Ask questions instead of making statements.** You may often find your child nodding or agreeing to statements while completely disengaging. This occurs because your child is passively listening. If the topic doesn't capture their interest, they see no reason to focus on it. Instead of making statements, try asking questions. This encourages your child to think about what you've said and consider the options, making them an active participant in the conversation.
- **Be soft and calm when talking.** Staying cool, calm, and collected is easier said than done. However, showing frustration or becoming agitated with your child may trigger their symptoms of ADHD and redirect their focus

to your emotional response rather than your words. Practicing self-control and emotional regulation is just as important for you as it is for your child. Harnessing the power of coping techniques and mindfulness will help you be more compassionate and provide reassurance during stressful outbursts or tantrums.

Practice makes perfect; healthy communication takes time and dedication. Choosing to wake up every day resilient and empowered to positively impact your child will bring genuine harmony to your relationship.

JOURNALING FOR SELF-REFLECTION

If you want your child to listen to you, you must listen to yourself. As parents, we often put self-care on the back burner. We can run around all day after everyone but ourselves, tired and drained as the night ends. With a simple five minutes of self-reflection, you can transform your relationships with yourself and with others. Once you've grabbed your journal and collected a pen, take some time to consider the following prompts:

1. How do you establish boundaries and prevent yourself from taking on someone else's emotions and stress?
2. What are your fears?
3. What activities would you like to do more often?
4. What activities would you prefer to do less frequently?
5. How have you grown or changed over the past two years?

ADVOCATE FOR YOUR CHILD'S EDUCATION

> *Kids with ADHD have to work very hard to achieve a grade most would consider mediocre. When I congratulate my son for getting a 75 (and, of course, discuss why he got the answers wrong that he did), it's because I know the hard work it took to achieve that passing grade.*
>
> — M.A.

Undoubtedly, school is one of the most challenging experiences we face. We've all felt the pressure of fitting in, making the right friends, and looking the part. On top of that, the mix of raging hormones and rapidly changing bodies causes a lot of confusion and anxiety. While some may find this easier to navigate than others, for children with ADHD, it is a whole other level of difficulty. While ADHD doesn't hold anyone back from succeeding, it can make it an uphill battle. With this being said, let's delve into this chapter and unlock the secret to success for your child's academic journey.

INDIVIDUALIZED EDUCATION PROGRAMS (IEPS)

Children with ADHD often need more support than others—a helping hand to boost their academics. The symptoms of ADHD, such as impulsivity and hyperactivity, can make learning extremely challenging, meaning there is no shame or guilt in seeking additional help and resources. The individualized education program (IEP) was invented to help children like yours succeed and achieve their goals. The program offers hands-on support for children with all kinds of disabilities—free of charge.

Picture an IEP as a written plan with legal rights, almost like a map that provides directions tailored to your child's needs and condition. It offers instructions, support, and all the services your child can use to boost their education. IEPs are covered by special education law, the Individuals with Disabilities Education Act (IDEA), and are only available to children who attend public school.

How Are IEP Services Offered?

In most cases, the services and goals outlined in an IEP can be provided within a general school environment, such as a regular classroom. For example, a reading teacher might assist a small group of students needing extra help while the rest of the class works with the regular teacher. This small group approach addresses the needs of students with similar challenges.

The best part about IEPs is that they don't isolate your child from others; they attempt to integrate students with disabilities alongside their peers. However, if the necessary level of support can't be provided in a general classroom, students may be placed in specialized learning classrooms. This may occur if your child needs complete silence and no distractions to complete a test or assignment. Teachers in these settings are typically trained to support children with special educational needs. Students in specialized classrooms spend most of their day there but join regular classes when possible, such as during lunch, gym, or art classes.

How Is an IEP Developed?

Understanding legal jargon has never been easy, but it may just be the thing that transforms your child's challenges into strengths. So, let's break down the IEP process and see how your child can receive the help they need!

Step One: A Referral or Request Is Made for an Evaluation

If your child exhibits concerning academic behavior, the referral process is initiated by a teacher, parent, or doctor. Don't be afraid to raise awareness and speak to your child's teacher, asking them to watch for any warning signs. The teacher then alerts the school counselor or psychologist, which involves collecting detailed information on your child's academic progress and challenges. This may include the following:

- Conferences with you and your child
- Classroom observations assessing attention, behavior, and work completion

Collecting data helps school officials determine the next steps. Sometimes, simple classroom strategy adjustments, such as new seating partners or reducing the intensity of the workload, can resolve the issue.

Step Two: Your Child Is Evaluated

If simple classroom adjustments don't suffice, an educational assessment is conducted to identify any specific learning disabilities or health impairments. As the parent, you can consent to your child's assessment by signing a permission form detailing the involved professionals and tests. These tests might measure academic skills (reading, math) or developmental skills (speech, language). The evaluation team may include the following:

- Classroom teachers
- Psychologists
- Physical and occupational therapists
- Speech therapists
- Special needs educators
- Vision or hearing specialists

An official ADHD diagnosis will help further this assessment, as it recognizes that your child has learning difficulties. Once the assessment is over, a comprehensive report is created, outlining the educational classification and necessary support. You can review this report before the IEP is developed, collaborating with the team to address any concerns.

Step Three: Eligibility Is Decided, and a Meeting Is Scheduled

Once your child has been found eligible for an IEP, a meeting is held involving you and the evaluation team. The team discusses your child's needs and sets specific, measurable short-term and yearly goals. Your input is essential, as you know your child best. Typically, the support services your child will receive consist of the following:

- Special education
- Speech, occupational, or physical therapy
- Counseling
- Medical services (e.g., vision and hearing therapy)
- Additional supports like transportation, test modifications, special programs, and transition planning from age fourteen

Some services might be integrated into classroom activities to prevent overwhelming your child, while others are delivered individually. For example, an occupational therapist may suggest classroom-wide handwriting strategies to support a child with fine motor issues.

Step Four: Your Child Is Re-evaluated

After one year, your child's IEP will be reviewed annually to update goals and ensure they receive the support they need. Adjustments can also be made anytime if needed, and you can request a meeting with the team to adjust services as necessary.

504 PLAN

Like an IEP, a 504 plan offers additional academic support to your child. The only difference is that 504 plans aren't part of special education; they fall under different laws and function differently. However, both aim to help students succeed in school.

A 504 plan gets its name from Section 504 of the Rehabilitation Act, which prohibits discrimination against individuals with disabilities in federally funded programs or activities, such as public schools and publicly funded private schools. This law ensures that students with disabilities like ADHD receive a free and appropriate education tailored to their needs, something every child deserves!

Creating a 504 Plan

The process starts when a parent, teacher, school staff member, health care provider, or therapist requests an evaluation for the student. Although each school manages 504 plans differently, most schools have a 504 team that typically includes the principal, teachers, a school nurse, a guidance counselor, or a psychologist. This team reviews your child's grades, test scores, medical records, and teacher reports to determine eligibility.

If your child qualifies, the 504 team collaborates with you to identify necessary support and resources for your child's success, which are then documented in the 504 plan. Typically, these accommodations include the following:

- Specific seating arrangements in the classroom
- Extended time for tests and assignments
- Use of speech-to-text software for writing
- Modified textbooks such as audiobooks
- Adjusted class schedules
- Oral testing
- Access to the nurse's office
- Occupational or physical therapy

The plan may offer other accommodations to remove learning barriers without altering the educational content. If you request accommodations that aren't feasible, the school may also suggest an alternative. The 504 plan should be reviewed at least once a year to ensure the accommodations remain effective and relevant to your child's needs.

ESTABLISHING PARENT-SCHOOL PARTNERSHIPS

As a parent, you play a key role in the development of your child's academic success; both you and your child's teacher are going to need to work together as a team!

According to the American Federation of Teachers (2023), students and teachers gain a multitude of benefits from having a positive relationship with their parents. It was reported that parents who frequently communicated with their child's teacher noticed several positive changes in their child, including increased motivation, improved academic success, better attendance, and the adoption of positive behaviors both in and out of the classroom. On the other hand, frequent communication with parents provides teachers with valuable insights into their students' triggers, behavioral patterns, and attitudes. Pointing out your child's needs and offering key information will equip the teacher with everything they need to help your child succeed.

I know how busy life gets, especially when you have a little one with ADHD running around. For this reason, I've made a super simple list to help you create a good parent-school partnership without the added stress:

- **Meet face-to-face with them.** Getting a head start never hurts anyone, especially when meeting your child's teacher. If you haven't met them yet, now would be an excellent time to organize a meeting. This way, you'll be able to provide a copy of your child's IEP/504 plan or discuss the potential of creating one.
- **Develop a communication plan.** Healthy communication is key, so you'll want to make sure you have the teachers' working hours written down as well as updated contact information. Try to come up with a communication plan

that works best for both of you, for instance, monthly emails or a face-to-face meeting every term.

- **Keep them informed.** As we know, ADHD symptoms vary in intensity and fluctuate depending on age, hormones, and emotional factors. Keeping the teacher updated on current symptom struggles will help them understand your child better and avoid disciplining them for symptoms often perceived as naughtiness.
- **Recognize their efforts**. Many of today's teachers are overworked and underpaid. They work long hours and have limited resources. It's important that you encourage your child's teacher as much as possible. Thank them for all of their hard work, compliment them on how great they are at their job, and do your best to make them feel valued and appreciated.

EDUCATION STARTS AT HOME

You and your child's teacher may have way more in common than you know; let me explain. When your child comes home with a rotten cold, you become the nurse; you're equipped with medicine, comfy pillows and blankets, and heartwarming meals that could make anyone better. When your child refuses to eat healthy food, you turn into a top-tier chef and nutritionist, stuffing veggies into beige and bland food and secretly watching them consume all the minerals and vitamins they need. And then, when your child has a play date, you suddenly become an events manager, park ranger, and maybe even an artist. So, when it comes to learning at home, you're going to have to step into the shoes of a teacher and do what you do best: teach!

Your child never stops learning from you. Regardless of their age, you remain their constant source of advice, skills, and values. In the grand scheme of things, a few spelling lessons and math classes are just the basics. Yet creating a positive learning environment in your home can quite literally set your child up for lifelong success. Let's take a look at how you can continue to encourage your child to learn both in and out of the classroom:

- **Provide access to books.** Reading is one of the best learning tools, as it improves vocabulary, literacy skills, memory, problem-solving abilities, focus, and general knowledge. Reading is also a relaxing activity that offers many benefits to your child's mental well-being. Ensuring that your child always has a new book to read and literary goals to meet will transform their academic level. You could try getting a library card for your family or swapping books with friends.
- **Create functional spaces for different activities.** When children have separate spaces for activities, they tend to be more inclined to use them. Keeping pens, pencils, and books all in one space will also reduce mess and clutter. Consider investing in a desk or table for your child to work at each day; bonus points if you have an empty room or corner of the house designated for learning.
- **Follow a daily routine.** Remember, children with ADHD thrive with consistency. A daily study routine set at certain times will help your child direct their focus to learning and allow them to run off as much energy as needed beforehand. Plus, routines also give your child a sense of control, reducing those pesky feelings of stress and anxiety.

- **Create a language-rich environment.** Talk, talk, talk, and talk! Talking with your child at any free moment, such as during bath times or while driving, eating, or doing laundry, extends their vocabulary and improves their listening skills.
- **Instill independence at home.** Can your child read a book, follow a routine, or complete healthy habits without your help? Or do they require your constant supervision and assistance? Depending on their age, your children should be able to carry out basic tasks independently. Try to stick to the principle of "don't do for your children what they can do for themselves." The more reliant your child is on you, the less capable they are as adults!

Children with ADHD encounter barriers in all elements of life, including school, social groups, clubs, and communities. Your home should be a place where your child feels understood, supported, and encouraged. By creating a nurturing environment, you can help reduce the pressure of these challenges and empower your child to thrive.

JOURNALING FOR SELF-REFLECTION

Throughout this chapter, we've worked on becoming a better advocate for your child, which involves understanding their unique needs, communicating effectively with others, and continuously seeking ways to support their growth. However, the journey does not stop here; you must be your child's biggest supporter today, tomorrow, and every day from now on. Here are five journaling prompts to help you on this journey.

1. What are my child's greatest strengths and interests? How can you use these to support their growth and development?
2. What challenges does your child face at home, at school, and in social settings? How can you address these challenges, and what solutions are available?
3. How effective is your current communication with your child's teachers and school staff? Are they aware of your child's ADHD diagnosis?
4. Reflect on a time when knowing more about your child's rights could have made a difference. How will you continue to educate yourself and ensure you are well-informed in the future?
5. Who are the key people in your child's support network, and how can you strengthen these relationships to support your child better?

HARNESS THE ADHD SUPERPOWERS

> *Kids have a lot of gifts from their ADHD: unending creativity, thinking outside the box, energy, enthusiasm, and passion for their interests.*
>
> — C.J.

If you think back to Chapter 1, we explored how your child's symptoms of ADHD are secretly a collection of awesome superpowers. But we never really had the chance to see how these superpowers can be used to their advantage. I'm not sure about you, but I think it would be a shame to let these superpowers go to waste; every child deserves to discover how their strengths can lead to lifelong success and incredible adventures. So, let's get to it!

HYPERFOCUS

If you didn't know it yet, hyperfocus is the extraordinary power to direct all your focus to one activity. Picture it as intense commitment and dedication, where your child pours their entire heart into one singular thing, blocking out any other distraction. Jealous much? Because I sure am!

The best way to harness hyperactivity is by teaching your child how to self-monitor. Self-monitoring is an executive function skill that allows them to understand what is happening in their body and environment. It's the ability to check in with your behavior, actions, and emotions to improve learning, communication, behavior, and so much more. Let's take a closer look at how this can be done:

- **Teach them to write down their goals.** Hyperfocus often occurs when engaging in a demanding task. Showing your child how to write down goals and tick off each one as it is completed will allow them to stay on track and increase their productivity.
- **Help them find the right timing.** If your child is hyperfocused on a particular activity, chances are they'll let time pass by as if it never existed. The downside is that this can lead to other tasks being forgotten about and a huge pileup of late or missed assignments. Clocks, timers, and schedules can help your little one stay on track and check back in with their environment.
- **Create a superhero support system.** Hyperfocus is both a blessing and a curse. It's incredibly beneficial for studying but can be extremely problematic when triggered by video games. The key is to create a support system aware of your child's hyperfocus tendencies. This can help them redirect their thoughts and energy to other projects. If your child is old enough, consider talking with them about possible triggers and gestures that can steer them away from the activity, such as a pat on the back or a small walk break.

CREATIVITY

What do you think Picasso, Richard Branson, Simon Biles, and Leonardo da Vinci have in common? If you said ADHD, well done. If you said enormous achievement and tremendous success, you're also correct!

ADHD and creativity are a powerful combination, with no limits or barriers to your child's potential. Look at the countless influencers, innovators, and visionaries with ADHD who have achieved global recognition for their unique perspectives. Children with ADHD think outside the box, offering ideas and thoughts that transcend societal norms. It's time for us to celebrate their originality and artistic flair so they can pave their own path in life full of fulfillment and joy. Here's how it's done:

- **Complete the hardest task second.** Unlike traditional advice telling you to complete the most important task first, ADHD brains often need a warmup to spark their interest and motivation. Once you've got the ball rolling with simple and creative tasks, they'll be ready to accomplish anything and everything in their day!
- **Tackle bite-size tasks.** No one enjoys feeling overwhelmed and stressed, especially not a kid trying to tackle a day's worth of projects and assignments. Working on tasks for 25 minutes, followed by a 5-minute break, will help your child maintain their creative flow and motivation. You'll also be able to avoid draining their hyperfocus and boost productivity.
- **Cut the noise and clear the clutter.** Whether you have ADHD or not, a chaotic environment is bound to be distracting. Minimizing mess and loud sounds will help your child harness their creativity and focus on the task at

hand. Consider designated spaces for creativity and noise-cancelling headphones.
- **Experiment.** If your child has a creative mind, why not experiment with mind mapping, journaling, and brainstorming? Blurting out all your thoughts, emotions, and ideas can often help with productivity.

HIGH ENERGY

As someone who takes an hour to wake up, along with a strong cup of caffeine, I'd love to know where kids with ADHD get their energy from! Their intense zest for life often gets a bad rep for being distracting or too much to handle in classrooms. This is exactly why we must find environments where our little ones' energy can thrive and flourish. After all, it is a superpower. Let's take a look at some of the best outlets for high energy:

- **Build things.** Whether it's stacking Lego, creating living room forts, or taping water bottles together to create an awesome rocket, building is a fun and engaging way for your child to release their energy. Plus, it strengthens executive function skills such as problem-solving and planning.
- **Try Boy Scouts and Girl Scouts.** These groups are designed for children to build social skills and tackle problems hands-on while getting tons of exercise. The scouts include both a mental and physical workout, allowing your little ball of energy to have fun with other kids!
- **Play sports that they like.** If you're looking for your child to run off some of that pent-up energy, then it's time to take them swimming, running, trampolining, playing

basketball, and pretty much any sport you can imagine. Seriously, nothing is better than sweating off the energy!
- **Let them help you.** I'm not saying your child should become your new housemaid, but a little help cleaning here and there never hurt anyone. If you tend to do a Sunday morning clean or happen to have a rainy day, try getting your child involved and letting them sweep the floor or wipe down the surfaces. Not only does it burn off some energy, but it also shows them the importance of organization and helping out around the house!

BUILDING THEIR SELF-ESTEEM

Children with ADHD face more obstacles than we realize; they're often rejected by peers at school, fail assignments after trying their best, and feel out of place in almost every scenario. Something tells me this burden is way too heavy for a child's shoulders. So, let's skip to the solution:

- **Recognize your child's successes—big or small.** Affirmations and encouragement are some of the easiest ways to rebuild your child's self-esteem. When you notice them doing well on a test, trying hard at homework, or being compassionate with their siblings, reward them. Success looks different in every household; no matter how big or small your child's achievement is, they deserve to feel supported.
- **Identify their strengths.** Every child has a hidden talent, whether it's singing, acting, or drawing; encourage them to seek out their strengths. Even if they haven't yet discovered it, try new hobbies and invest in creative outlets for your child's emotions and behavior. Who

knows, you may find your child is the next Einstein or Picasso!
- **Build a connection with your child.** Numerous experts have emphasized just how important it is to have a strong bond with your child; it's one of the most crucial actions parents can take. Offering your child reassurance and reminding them of your unconditional love and support can equip them to better navigate potential rejections they may encounter.
- **Highlight their superpowers.** Educating your child about their ADHD diagnosis can be more empowering than you might think. ADHD doesn't have to be seen as a negative; it brings a range of unique strengths that can benefit them in many ways. Your role is to help them recognize and embrace these strengths and show them how to harness their superpower.

JOURNALING FOR SELF-REFLECTION

Understanding ADHD makes a world of difference; suddenly, all of those symptoms you once considered a burden to your child become a huge advantage. Below, you will find five journaling prompts based on this chapter. You can even invite your child to sit down and reflect with you. After all, you will need a lot of teamwork to build a happy and fulfilling future for your child. But don't worry; I know you'll do an excellent job!

Reflect on the following journaling prompts:

1. Reflect on a recent situation where you witnessed your child's unique strengths or abilities related to their ADHD. How did it make you feel, and how do you think it made them feel?

2. Think about a challenge your child faced recently. How did they approach it differently from others? What positive outcomes came from their approach?
3. Write about a time when you noticed your child's hyperfocus on something they are passionate about. How can you encourage and support this passion?
4. Consider the feedback you've received from teachers or caregivers about your child's behavior. How can you reframe any negative feedback into recognizing their strengths?
5. Imagine your child as an adult using their ADHD strengths in a career or hobby. What do you envision, and how can you help them work toward that future?

FAMILY FORTITUDE

> *Being a family means you are a part of something very wonderful. It means you will love and be loved for the rest of your life.*
>
> — LISA WEED

As we come to the end of our journey, it's a perfect time for us to express some gratitude, especially for the unconditional love and support we're blessed with. Whether you are married, in a relationship, or single, there will always be one heartbeat that loves you endlessly, looking to you for inspiration, strength, and guidance. That little voice that calls out for you, no matter how frustrated, sad, or exhausted they may be, is a constant reminder of your profound impact on their life. Let's cherish these moments, continue nurturing our relationships, and embrace the incredible role we have in shaping the future of someone truly magnificent.

HOW ADHD PLAYS INTO PARENT/CHILD RELATIONSHIPS

The most important relationship your child has is the one they have with you. A child's relationship with their parents can influence their perspective of other people and their view of their environment. Your little one grows and changes rapidly during those fundamental childhood years, which can feel scary and unfamiliar. As a parent, you become a source of safety, security, and love for your child. Whether you reciprocate those feelings or not, this relationship forms the foundation for their relationships throughout life. Without putting too much pressure on you, it's important to understand that you play a crucial role in your child's ability to develop and maintain healthy relationships.

So, what can you do to ensure a healthy, strong, and loving relationship with your child? Let's find out:

- **Have open and honest conversations.** At times, parenting ADHD can be just as stressful as having it. Hence, you both must understand the value of your relationship and work together to find effective strategies. When a routine or schedule doesn't work, tackle it differently. If symptoms are constantly fluctuating, then find holistic solutions as a team. Have an open and honest conversation with your child.
- **Listen and empathize.** Healthy communication begins by listening. Remember, your child is still learning and growing every day, so there are many situations they won't know how to handle correctly and emotions that will feel too heavy to manage. Have an open heart, show reassurance, and acknowledge what they have to say.

- **Set realistic expectations.** Your child is still a child. No matter how many open and honest conversations you have or how many strategies you implement, you have to remember that kids make silly mistakes. They'll scream, cry, and insult you till the Earth's end, but trust me, they need you more than ever in those moments. Keep your hopes high but expectations realistic; we're not aiming for perfection, just improvement.
- **Show your love and say it often.** We expect our children to know we love them, but actions don't actually speak louder than words in this case. Children with ADHD often misinterpret words and don't pick up on cues or gestures. Hence, it's always best to affirm your love through words. Even if your child is screaming, crying, and throwing a hissy fit, saying "I love you" is the best call of action.

BALANCING SIBLING RELATIONSHIPS

Can ADHD drain and strain sibling relationships? Well, the truth is, yes, it can!

Whether your child has ADHD or not, arguments and disagreements are inevitable. However, many parents may not realize that the non-ADHD sibling often feels immense pressure to be the "good" kid. When one child is acting out, being reckless, and getting bad grades, the other sibling may feel like they have little room to make the typical mistakes of tweens and teens. If you and your partner lead busy lives, this dynamic can create an attention battle between the siblings, further straining their relationship.

Just by scratching the surface, we can see a lot of potential for resentment and envy to build up over time. To avoid this, you have to take a more balanced parenting approach and fortify the sibling relationship. Try to implement a few of these strategies:

- **Orchestrate fun family activities.** Getting outside and having some fun can really switch up a negative dynamic. Try taking your entire family to play mini golf, go on a hike, or visit the cinema. You could even create a family ritual, play board games, or watch a movie every Sunday evening!
- **Create outlets for frustration.** Remember, kids with ADHD often struggle with managing their emotions and actions as a result of their executive dysfunction. This means that it can often lead to them lashing out at siblings. As parents, you must find other ways for them to release their frustrations. Simple physical outlets like a basketball hoop, indoor bike, or trampoline can be great for this. Also, proper ADHD treatment, including medication and family therapy, can help.
- **Prioritize quality time.** Make sure to spend some one-on-one time with each child every day. Whether you're working on a house project, cooking, or running errands, this focused attention can really strengthen your bond and boost your self-esteem. Every minute counts!
- **Keep things fair.** Whether it's routines, rewards, or consequences, keeping the rules and regulations of your house fair and equal will create a peaceful household. If one child is punished for missing out on their chores but the other isn't, it will clearly create an unfair dynamic, leading to further resentment. Ensuring everything is written down and the entire family is on the same page will help tremendously. You can even check in with each other once a month to see if any adjustments need to be made!

STRENGTHENING PARTNERSHIPS AS PARENTS

While you may not want to hear this, having a child with ADHD can really shake up a marriage or partnership. The constant stress from managing their behavior and emotional ups and downs can put a strain on your relationship. Plus, one parent often ends up shouldering more of the caregiving duties, leading to feelings of imbalance and resentment. And let's not forget the clash of parenting styles—disagreements on how to handle situations can be a big source of tension!

Every relationship has its highs and lows; what truly matters is how you handle those moments. Let's take a look at a few strategies for reconnecting in stressful times:

- **Agree on structure and routine.** Recognize that agreeing on structure and routines for ADHD can be a process that requires patience and understanding. It's common for parents to have different views initially, even when it comes to getting a diagnosis, so allowing each other time to come to terms with the new strategies and concepts is crucial.
- **Be open-minded.** Respect each other's perspectives and feelings, or you'll end up in a constant cycle of avoidance and disagreements. The best way to do this is by using open and honest communication; speak up about your concerns, fears, and worries. Then, as a team, work together to find strategies and solutions that fit the entire family. You can also consider seeking a second opinion from a healthcare professional if there are uncertainties or disagreements.

- **Spend quality time.** Make time for each other as a couple. You and your partner must spend regular time together to strengthen your relationship. If you've had disagreements and feel distant, reconnect by going on a movie date or revisiting activities you both enjoy.

JOURNALING FOR SELF-REFLECTION

And just like that, we've reached the end of our journey, but just before we say goodbye, let's take a moment to acknowledge and embrace gratitude. Use the journaling prompts below to guide you:

1. Reflect on the most significant thing you learned about your child's ADHD. How has this understanding changed your perspective and approach?
2. Write about a specific moment when you felt particularly grateful for your child's progress. What emotions did you experience, and how did this moment impact your relationship?
3. List three things you are thankful for concerning your child's unique qualities and strengths related to their ADHD. How do these qualities enrich your family life?
4. Describe a time when your child's resilience or creativity amazed you. How did this moment help you appreciate their ADHD as a source of strength rather than a challenge?
5. Consider the support systems (family, friends, teachers, or professionals) that have helped you and your child along this journey. How have they contributed to your understanding and gratitude? Write a thank you note to these individuals.

Your Chance to Help Other Parents Like You

You're going to notice more and more harmony in your home as you implement these changes, and your child will thrive... who better to inspire other parents than someone who's witnessing this transformation firsthand?

Simply by sharing your honest opinion of this book and a little about how it has helped your family, you'll show other parents where they can find the guidance they've been longing for, and you'll inspire them to implement these changes themselves.

WANT TO HELP OTHERS?

Thank you so much for your support. I wish you and your family all the happiness in the world going forward.

>>> **Click here to leave your review on Amazon.**

CONCLUSION

Just like that, we reached the end of our journey. I can't believe you've come this far; look at how much your family's life has transformed!

Not only have you unlocked a holistic approach that combines evidence-based strategies and practical tips, but you now know how to support your child's ADHD journey. For instance, you've learned about the importance of setting clear expectations and providing positive reinforcement. I bet that feels amazing, doesn't it?

You've embraced a truly unique parenting approach, one that tailors interventions specifically to your child's unique strengths and challenges. This approach incorporates empowering techniques like behavior modifications, mindfulness practices, and enhanced communication skills. Unlike other methods that might focus narrowly on medication or single solutions, you now have a comprehensive toolkit that dives deep into all of the aspects of parenting a child with ADHD. Seriously, you've completely revolutionized the parenting game!

Most importantly, you understand how to nurture your child's emotional well-being, boost their self-esteem, and create harmony within your family dynamics. You can wave goodbye to sibling rivalries and parenting disputes as you integrate practical schedules and routines that complement your family's needs. I bet your house is warmer than ever, filled with love, compassion, and care for one another.

As you continue working toward building a solid foundation for your child's future and implementing these strategies, I want you to envision the positive changes ahead. There will be tough times and days when you'll feel too exhausted to try. But remember, the benefits outweigh the tantrums, academic difficulties, impulsivity, and inattentiveness. A stronger connection with your child, newfound resilience in facing challenges, and a deepened sense of confidence as a parent to a child with ADHD will leave you feeling more empowered than ever before.

By embracing and nurturing your child's emotional growth, strengthening the bonds within your family, and channeling their energy into positive outlets, you're paving the path for long-term success and fulfillment. After all, this journey wasn't just about finding solutions; it was about igniting lasting progress and resilience in both your child and your family. I honestly can't wait to hear all about it. I bet your little one has started their morning routine, haven't they? Has their teacher noticed an improvement in their executive functioning skills yet? Did you set up a 504 plan already? Do you feel that you've grown and improved as a parent? There's so much you have to tell; we're all waiting to hear your story!

As each day approaches, keep moving forward by implementing the strategies you've learned, seeking support when needed, and celebrating your entire family's successes. Know and trust that every step brings you closer to a brighter and more fulfilling future together as a team. It seems like your child isn't the only superhero in the family—well done!

REFERENCES

"Every Creative With ADHD Should Know These 14 Tips For A Happier Work Life," n.d. https://www.linkedin.com/pulse/every-creative-adhd-should-know-14-tips-happier-work-life-hunt.

"Health Effects Assessment: Potential Neurobehavioral Effects of Synthetic Food Dyes in Children." Office of Environmental Health Hazard Assessment, August 2020. https://oehha.ca.gov/media/downloads/risk-assessment/report/food dyesassessmentdraft082820.pdf.

Ad4pT4ble. "Why Is an ADHD Diagnosis Important for a Child?" The Autism Service, November 28, 2022. https://www.theautismservice.co.uk/news/why-is-an-adhd-diagnosis-important-for-a-child/.

ADDA Editorial Team. "ADHD Time Blindness: How to Detect It & Regain Control Over Time." *ADDA - Attention Deficit Disorder Association* (blog), October 2, 2023. https://add.org/adhd-time-blindness/.

ADDitude Editors. "Hyperfocus: How to Control Your ADHD Focus." ADDitude, n.d. https://www.additudemag.com/slideshows/hyperfocus-for-productivity/.

ADDitude. "The Messy Bedroom (and Backpack) Cure for Kids with ADHD," June 21, 2021. https://www.additudemag.com/slideshows/messy-bedroom-organi zation-tips-adhd-kids/#:

ADHD Centre. "6 Ways To Improve Communication With Kids With ADHD." The ADHD Centre, February 22, 2021. https://www.adhdcentre.co.uk/6-ways-to-improve-communication-with-kids-with-adhd/.

ADHD Centre. "What Is Inattentive ADHD and How Does It Affect Your Children?" The ADHD Centre, October 6, 2017. https://www.adhdcentre.co. uk/inattentive-adhd-affect-children/.

admin. "How to Make a Visual Schedule for Your Child." *KidsFirst* (blog), December 22, 2014. https://kids-first.com.au/how-to-make-a-visual-sched ule-for-your-child/.

Administrator. "Improve Your Child's Active Listening Skills." Oxford Learning, June 13, 2017. https://www.oxfordlearning.com/improve-active-listening-skills/.

American Federation of Teachers. "Building Parent-Teacher Relationships." Reading Rockets, n.d. https://www.readingrockets.org/topics/parent-engage ment/articles/building-parent-teacher-relationships.

REFERENCES

APA PsycNet. "APA PsycNet," n.d. https://psycnet.apa.org/doiLanding?doi=10.1037%2F0893-3200.16.4.381.

Arnold, L. Eugene, Nicholas Lofthouse, and Elizabeth Hurt. "Artificial Food Colors and Attention-Deficit/Hyperactivity Symptoms: Conclusions to Dye For." *Neurotherapeutics* 9, no. 3 (July 2012): 599–609. https://doi.org/10.1007/s13311-012-0133-x.

Attention deficit hyperactivity disorder: How common is it?" NICE. Last modified April 2024. https://cks.nice.org.uk/topics/attention-deficit-hyperactivity-disorder/background-information/prevalence/.

Attitude Editors. "Who Can Diagnose ADHD or ADD? Doctors, Psychologists, & More." ADDitude, April 8, 2024. https://www.additudemag.com/who-can-diagnose-adhd/.

Bachrach, Stephen. "504 Education Plans (for Parents)." KidsHealth, 2016. https://kidshealth.org/en/parents/504-plans.html.

Bean, Sara. "Behavioral Triggers: How to Find the Ones That Set Your Kid Off." Empowering Parents, 2011. https://www.empoweringparents.com/article/how-to-find-the-behavioral-triggers-that-set-your-kid-off/.

Beck, Colleen. "Self-Monitoring Strategies for Kids." *The OT Toolbox* (blog), May 3, 2021. https://www.theottoolbox.com/self-monitoring-strategies-for-kids/.

Bertin, Mark. "How ADHD Impacts Your Child's Communication Skills – and 11 Ways to Help." ADDitude, May 31, 2022. https://www.additudemag.com/communication-skills-for-kids-adhd/.

Blanchfield, Theodora. "How Does Caffeine Affect People with ADHD?" Verywell Mind, n.d. https://www.verywellmind.com/how-does-caffeine-affect-people-with-adhd-5217867.

Blanchfield, Theodora. "Types of Therapy for ADHD." Verywell Mind, n.d. https://www.verywellmind.com/types-of-therapy-for-adhd-5272434.

Bleeker, Sydney. "12 Powerful Quotes from Parents of Kids with ADHD." *The Healthy* (blog), n.d. https://www.thehealthy.com/adhd/quotes-adhd-parents-kids/.

Bleeker, Sydney. "12 Powerful Quotes from Parents of Kids with ADHD." *The Healthy* (blog), n.d. https://www.thehealthy.com/adhd/quotes-adhd-parents-kids/.

Brain Balance. "Common Challenges of Parenting a Child With Challenges," n.d. https://www.brainbalancecenters.com/blog/common-challenges-of-parenting-a-child-with-adhd-dyslexia-or-learning-differences.

Brain Balance. "Tips for Building an Effective Relationship with Your Child's Teachers," n.d. https://www.brainbalancecenters.com/blog/tips-building-effective-relationship-childs-teachers.

Buzanko, Dr Caroline. "How to Manage Impulsive Behaviours in Kids with

ADHD." *Dr. Caroline Buzanko* (blog), September 27, 2019. https://drcarolineb uzanko.com/how-to-manage-impulsive-behaviours-in-kids-with-adhd/.

Causbie, Kate. "4 Ways to Practice Empathetic Parenting." CampKindnessCounts, April 1, 2018. https://www.campkindnesscounts.org/single-post/2018/03/31/4-ways-to-practice-empathetic-parenting.

CDC. "About Attention-Deficit / Hyperactivity Disorder (ADHD)." Centers for Disease Control and Prevention, June 27, 2024. https://www.cdc.gov/adhd/about/index.html.

CDC. "Protecting the Health of Children with ADHD." Centers for Disease Control and Prevention, May 15, 2024. https://www.cdc.gov/adhd/articles/protecting-the-health-of-children.html.

Cuncic, Arlin. "7 Active Listening Techniques to Practice in Your Daily Conversations." Verywell Mind, 2024. https://www.verywellmind.com/what-is-active-listening-3024343.

Dahl, Danielle. "80 ADHD Quotes About the Neurodivergent Way of Paying Attention." Everyday Power, April 8, 2023. https://everydaypower.com/adhd-quotes/.

DCD. "Data and Statistics on ADHD." CDC. Attention-Deficit / Hyperactivity Disorder (ADHD), May 23, 2024. https://www.cdc.gov/adhd/data/index.html.

Delap, Ellen. "How Do You Create a Daily Routine for a Child with ADHD?" LinkedIn, January 17, 2024. https://www.linkedin.com/advice/0/how-do-you-create-daily-routine-child-adhd.

Dorn, Paige. "8 Ways to Strengthen a Parent-Child Relationship." Family Services, July 28, 2020. https://www.familyservicesnew.org/news/8-ways-to-strengthen-a-parent-child-relationship/.

Ellis, Rachel Reiff. "How ADHD Can Impact Your Child's Sleep." WebMD, n.d. https://www.webmd.com/add-adhd/childhood-adhd/adhd-child-sleep.

Emily. "How To Discipline A Child With ADHD." *Goally Apps & Tablets for Kids* (blog), May 31, 2023. https://getgoally.com/blog/how-to-discipline-a-child-with-adhd/.

Fosco, Whitney D, Larry W Hawk, Keri S Rosch, and Michelle G Bubnik. "Evaluating Cognitive and Motivational Accounts of Greater Reinforcement Effects among Children with Attention-Deficit/Hyperactivity Disorder." *Behavioral and Brain Functions* 11, no. 1 (December 2015): 20. https://doi.org/10.1186/s12993-015-0065-9.

Fye, Devon. "Focus Supplements and Vitamins for ADHD: Zinc, Iron, Magnesium." ADDitude, April 11, 2017. https://www.additudemag.com/treatment/vitamins-and-supplements/.

Gerten, Katie. "16 Quotes That Illustrate ADHD." *Youth Dynamics | Mental Health Care for Montana Kids* (blog), October 10, 2022. https://www.youthdynamics.

org/16-quotes-that-illustrate-adhd/.

Goally. "What Is The Best Parenting Style For ADHD?" *Goally Apps & Tablets for Kids* (blog), May 17, 2024. https://getgoally.com/blog/what-is-the-best-parenting-style-for-adhd/.

Green, Rachael. "ADHD Symptom Spotlight: Emotional Dysregulation." Verywell Mind, December 21, 2023. https://www.verywellmind.com/adhd-symptom-spotlight-emotional-dysregulation-5219946.

Grushkin, Beth. "Showing Empathy to Kids With ADHD." Fuzzymama, January 15, 2020. https://www.fuzzymama.com/showing-empathy-kids-adhd/.

Hasan, Shirin. "Therapy for ADHD (for Parents)," 2017. https://kidshealth.org/en/parents/adhd-therapy.html.

Hatfield, Heather. "When Your Child's ADHD Affects You as a Couple." WebMD, n.d. https://www.webmd.com/add-adhd/childhood-adhd/features/child-adhd-parental-relationship.

Healthline. "What Is Executive Dysfunction? Causes, Diagnosis, Treatment," April 12, 2018. https://www.healthline.com/health/executive-dysfunction.

Hebert, Jackie. "ADHD and Emotional Dysregulation: Signs & How To Improve." Beyond Booksmart, March 17, 2023. https://www.beyondbooksmart.com/executive-functioning-strategies-blog/adhd-emotional-dysregulation.

Hunt, Tristan. "Every Creative With ADHD Should Know These 14 Tips For A Happier Work Life." LinkedIn, May 10, 2022. https://www.linkedin.com/pulse/every-creative-adhd-should-know-14-tips-happier-work-life-hunt.

Jackson, Marie. "Kids' Room Ideas from a Professional Organizer." ADDitude, n.d. https://www.additudemag.com/kids-room-ideas-adhd-child/.

Jones, Heather. "Do ADHD Symptoms Differ in Boys and Girls?" Verywell Health, n.d. https://www.verywellhealth.com/do-adhd-symptoms-differ-in-boys-and-girls-5207995.

KidsHealth. "ADHD In Kids (for Parents)," n.d. https://kidshealth.org/en/parents/adhd.html.

KidsHealth. "ADHD Medicines (for Parents)," n.d. https://kidshealth.org/en/parents/adhd-medicines.html.

Kingsley, Ellen. "Easy Mindfulness Exercises for Kids with ADHD." ADDituteMag.com, 2007. https://utahparentcenter.org/wp-content/uploads/2020/04/Easy-Mindfulness-Exercises-for-Kids-with-ADHD.pdf.

KneeTie. "Navigating the Waters: Understanding ADHD and Parenting Challenges." LinkedIn, February 28, 2024. https://www.linkedin.com/pulse/navigating-waters-understanding-adhd-parenting-challenges-kneetie-r5zec.

Lee Andrew. "12 Quotes To Help Parents Managing Children With ADHD Through The Day." Reader's Digest Asia, n.d. https://www.rdasia.com/true-stories-lifestyle/12-quotes-help-parents-managing-children-adhd-through-day/.

Lee, Yi-Chen, Chyi-Rong Chen, and Keh-Chung Lin. "Effects of Mindfulness-Based Interventions in Children and Adolescents with ADHD: A Systematic Review and Meta-Analysis of Randomized Controlled Trials." *International Journal of Environmental Research and Public Health* 19, no. 22 (November 17, 2022): 15198. https://doi.org/10.3390/ijerph192215198.

Lillis, Charlotte. "ADHD Triggers: What to Know." MedicalNewsToay, July 26, 2019. https://www.medicalnewstoday.com/articles/325867.

Linda. "How to Use Visuals for Children & Adolescents with ADHD." ADHD Done Differently, February 5, 2021. https://adhddonedifferently.com.au/2021/02/05/how-to-use-visuals-children-with-adhd/.

Lopatin, Alla. "ADHD and Time Blindness: 3 Ways to Help Your Child or Teen Manage Their Time." *Dr. Sharon Saline* (blog), July 24, 2023. https://drsharonsaline.com/2023/07/24/adhd-and-time-blindness-3-ways-to-help-your-child-or-teen-manage-their-time/.

Low, Keath. "Why Kids With ADHD Need Structure (And How to Provide It)." Verywell Mind, April 19, 2022. https://www.verywellmind.com/why-is-structure-important-for-kids-with-adhd-20747.

masterdaniel. "How to Improve Listening Skills in Children with ADHD and Autism." Special Strong, May 14, 2024. https://www.specialstrong.com/how-to-improve-listening-skills-in-children-with-adhd-and-autism/.

Mayo Clinic. "Attention-Deficit/Hyperactivity Disorder (ADHD) in Children - Symptoms and Causes," n.d. https://www.mayoclinic.org/diseases-conditions/adhd/symptoms-causes/syc-20350889.

McIlroy, Tanja. "21 Ways to Create a Positive Learning Environment at Home." *Empowered Parents* (blog), March 26, 2021. https://empoweredparents.co/learning-environment-at-home/.

Melissa. "Material Share Monday: 5 Finger Breathing." *The Calming Corner* (blog), November 4, 2018. https://www.thecalmcorner.com/2018/11/material-share-monday-5-finger-breathing.html.

Miller, Gia. "ADHD Parenting: 12 Tips to Tackle Common Challenges." PsychCentral, May 17, 2016. https://psychcentral.com/childhood-adhd/parenting-kids-with-adhd-tips-to-tackle-common-challenges.

Morin, Amy. "Ways to Help Your Child Gain Better Impulse Control." Parents, June 18, 2024. https://www.parents.com/ways-to-teach-children-impulse-control-1095035.

National Institute of Mental Health (NIMH). "Attention-Deficit/Hyperactivity Disorder," n.d. https://www.nimh.nih.gov/health/topics/attention-deficit-hyperactivity-disorder-adhd.

Neelkant. "Learning Begins At Home & Progresses In School." *Meru International*

146 | REFERENCES

School (blog), January 30, 2020. https://meruinternationalschool.com/blog/learning-begins-at-home-progresses-in-school/.

NHS. "Attention Deficit Hyperactivity Disorder (ADHD) - Symptoms," October 20, 2017. https://www.nhs.uk/conditions/attention-deficit-hyperactivity-disorder-adhd/symptoms/.

Nigg, Joel. "Emotional Resilience with ADHD: Coping with Dysregulated Feelings." ADDitude, June 11, 2024. https://www.additudemag.com/emotional-resilience-adhd-coping/.

Novick, Ilana. "Parent's Quick Guide for Disciplining Kids Who Have ADHD." Psych Central, September 7, 2018. https://psychcentral.com/adhd/parents-guide-for-disciplining-kids-with-adhd.

O'Shea, Colleen. "Individualized Education Programs (IEPs) (for Parents)." KidsHealth, 2022. https://kidshealth.org/en/parents/iep.html.

Parker, Catherine. "Improving Communication Skills with ADHD Children." LinkedIn, June 8, 2017. https://www.linkedin.com/pulse/improving-communication-skills-adhd-children-catherine-parker.

PhD, Richard E. A. Loren. "Steps to Help Kids with ADHD Manage Their Emotional Outbursts." Cincinnati Children's Blog, October 8, 2019. https://blog.cincinnatichildrens.org/healthy-living/child-development-and-behavior/steps-to-help-kids-with-adhd-manage-their-emotional-outbursts/.

Porter, Eloise. "Learn the Triggers for Your ADHD Symptoms." Healthline, December 17, 2012. https://www.healthline.com/health/adhd/adhd-trigger-symptoms.

Preiato, Daniel. "ADHD and Exercise: What You Need to Know." Healthline, October 19, 2021. https://www.healthline.com/health/fitness/adhd-and-exercise.

Preiato, Daniel. "ADHD and Exercise: What You Need to Know." Healthline, October 19, 2021. https://www.healthline.com/health/fitness/adhd-and-exercise.

Psychology Today Staff. "Emotion Regulation." Psychology Today, n.d. https://www.psychologytoday.com/us/basics/emotion-regulation.

Resnick, Ariane. "ADHD Diet for Kids: Foods to Eat and Foods to Avoid." Verywell Mind, n.d. https://www.verywellmind.com/adhd-diet-for-kids-foods-to-eat-and-foods-to-avoid-5225681.

Runcan, Patricia Luciana, Corneliu Constantineanu, Brigitta Ielics, and Dorin Popa. "The Role of Communication in the Parent-Child Interaction." *Procedia - Social and Behavioral Sciences* 46 (2012): 904–8. https://doi.org/10.1016/j.sbspro.2012.05.221.

Russell, Dr Lucy. "5 ADHD Strengths To Harness In Your Child." They Are The

Future, May 31, 2023. https://www.theyarethefuture.co.uk/adhd-strengths-in-your-child/.

Saline, Dr. Sharon. "Consistent Parenting in ADHD Families: A 5-Step Plan for Improving Cooperation and Communication." *Dr. Sharon Saline* (blog), April 30, 2022. https://drsharonsaline.com/2022/04/30/consistent-parenting-in-adhd-families-a-5-step-plan-for-improving-cooperation-and-communication/.

Saline, Sharon. "Sibling Relationships and ADHD: How to Mend Family Conflict." ADDitude, July 7, 2021. https://www.additudemag.com/sibling-relationships-adhd-families/.

Scott, Elizabeth. "8 Traits That Can Make You More Emotionally Resilient." Verywell Mind, April 28, 2020. https://www.verywellmind.com/emotional-resilience-is-a-trait-you-can-develop-3145235.

Shenfield, Dr Tali. "Understanding the Emotional Aspects of ADHD." Child Psychology Resources by Dr. Tali Shenfield, November 8, 2018. https://www.psy-ed.com/wpblog/emotional-aspects-of-adhd/.

Shutterfly Community. "55 Family Quotes and Family Sayings." Shutterfly, May 31, 2024. https://www.shutterfly.com/ideas/family-quotes/.

Sreenivas, Shishira. "ADHD and Your Child's Self-Esteem." WebMD, n.d. https://www.webmd.com/add-adhd/features/adhd-and-child-self-esteem.

Tartakovsky, Margarita, and Christina Ward. "ADHD Meltdowns: 9 Tips to Deal with Tantrums." Psych Central, May 17, 2016. https://psychcentral.com/childhood-adhd/adhd-kids-9-tips-to-tame-tantrums.

"The Power of Community Quotes." A Global Professional Women's Network | Ellevate. Last modified February 3, 2021. https://www.ellevatenetwork.com/articles/8538-quotes-about-the-power-of-community.

The Understood Team. "What Is a 504 Plan?" Understood, n.d. https://www.understood.org/en/articles/what-is-a-504-plan.

Time Timer. "Routines to Set Children with ADHD up for Success at Home," October 21, 2021. https://www.timetimer.com/blogs/news/routines-to-set-children-with-adhd-up-for-success-at-home.

Turner, Lauren. Twinkle, October 3, 2022. https://www.twinkl.com.ph/blog/the-importance-of-a-daily-schedule-for-a-child-with-adhd.

Understood. "Dad of a 4-Year-Old with ADHD (James' Story)," n.d. https://www.understood.org/en/podcasts/adhd-aha/preschool-adhd-parenting-story.

Villines, Zawn. "Tantrums and ADHD: Causes and How to Deal with Them." MedicalNewsToday, July 9, 2021. https://www.medicalnewstoday.com/articles/tantrums-and-adhd.

Wajszilber, Dafna, José Arturo Santisteban, and Reut Gruber. "Sleep Disorders in Patients with ADHD: Impact and Management Challenges." *Nature and Science of Sleep* 10, no. December (2018): 453–80. https://doi.org/10.2147/nss.s163074.

Watson, Stephanie. "ADHD Inattentive Type: Symptoms, Causes, and Treatment." WebMD, n.d. https://www.webmd.com/add-adhd/childhood-adhd/adhd-inattentive-type.

West, Mary. "Losing Patience with a Child with ADHD: Coping Strategies and Tips," June 28, 2023. https://www.medicalnewstoday.com/articles/i-have-no-patience-for-my-adhd-child.

Wilkins, Faith. "How Is the ADHD Brain Different?" Child Mind Institute, n.d. https://childmind.org/article/how-is-the-adhd-brain-different/.

Wymbs, Brian T., William E. Pelham, Brooke S. G. Molina, Elizabeth M. Gnagy, Tracey K. Wilson, and Joel B. Greenhouse. "Rate and Predictors of Divorce among Parents of Youths with ADHD." *Journal of Consulting and Clinical Psychology* 76, no. 5 (2008): 735–44. https://doi.org/10.1037/a0012719.

Printed in Great Britain
by Amazon